JOHN K. AMANCHUKWU SR.

ERACED

UNCOVERING THE LIES OF CRITICAL RACE THEORY AND ABORTION

IKG Global, LLC

PO Box 114

Rolesville, NC 27571-0114

ISBN: 978-0-578-39517-3

Publishing services provided by BelieversBookServices.com, with John R. Greco

Cover Design by CU Creative Co. Copyright © 2022. All rights reserved.

Some of the anecdotal illustrations in this book are true to life and are included with permission of the persons involved. All other illustrations are composites of real situations, and any resemblance to people living or dead is coincidental.

First Printing: April 2022

Printed in The United States of America

❀ Created with Vellum

This book is dedicated to TEAM Amanchukwu, the fruit and posterity of the Wooden, Weeks, and McNeil families.

To my loving, caring, strong, fervent, virtuous, and bonny wife, Crystal, I salute you for your unfailing support and diligence in being the consummate homemaker while working outside of the home. You are to be commended, revered, and honored, for you're irreplaceable in our family. May we grow old together and drive slow upon busy roads in the distant future. My love for you endures a lifetime.

To John Patrick, my oldest child who made me a proud father first; to Pamelyn Jewel, who will be Daddy's princess forever; and to John Jr., aka "Spiderman," keep webbing the villains of this age and foes to come—may the words and truth that emanate from these pages be a guidepost for the legacy of the Amanchukwu family. Your name has great meaning: Amanchukwu means I know God, and it's my prayer and commitment that you serve the God of the Bible for all your days.

CONTENTS

INTRODUCTION

Something is terribly wrong in our world. But I don't need to tell you that. Every time you turn on the television or scroll through social media, you can see it for yourself. You've probably seen it at work and in your local schools as well. In fact, you've likely experienced it firsthand.

I'm talking about racism.

Racism is, of course, nothing new in the United States of America. Our history is blotted and marred with slavery, the KKK, and Jim Crow, among other horrors. But today's brand of racism is different: it's more subtle but just as damaging. The racism of today attempts to murder our children in the womb in the name of choice, poison the minds of those who escape in the name of education, and sentence the rest of the black community to lives of victimhood in the name of justice, all while flipping the sharp edge of racism around to stab whites of every socio-economic background.

In the world progressives imagine, nearly everything is racist, and anyone who disagrees with their views are racists. They have no desire to see Martin Luther King Jr.'s dream come true; they have no wish to see people of all colors and creeds come together as one American people. Instead, they hope to see tribal divisions grow and violence in the streets continue. In fact, they long to undo the progress we've made since the Civil Rights Act was first passed in 1964. They talk about equity but never equality. They shout about social justice but are silent about actual justice when the suspect's skin color doesn't fit their narrative. And they say they care about the lives of black people, even as they support policies that make abortion the number-one cause of death for black Americans.

Abortion and critical race theory are poisonous plants that both grow from the bitter soil of racism, and I believe they are among the greatest evils persisting in our time. The pro-life cause has been on the hearts of most white evangelicals since the *Roe v. Wade* Supreme Court decision of 1973. Sadly, it has not been embraced to the same degree by black Christians, though I hope to change that. Critical race theory is a newer plague, and while some believers are beginning to understand the harm it is doing to our society, many others have embraced it as a more righteous way of viewing our world.

I am a black man, a husband, a father, a minister of the gospel, and a disciple of Jesus Christ. I can no longer sit idly by while these despicable forms of racism continue to fester and grow, threatening my family, my community, and the country that I love. That is why I started **ERACED, a movement that loves life of every race and color, and sees all mankind, born and unborn, as one blood and equally valuable.** In this book you hold in your hands, we'll walk through a bit of the history behind critical race theory and the abortion industry. We'll also survey the damage being done to black communities and to our nation at large. In addition, we'll take a look at what Scripture has to say about these issues. Finally, we'll talk a bit about what we can do to get off the destructive path we're currently racing down.

I don't know what brought you to this book or what your background may be, but my prayer is that as you read, your eyes will be opened to the darkness that lies beneath critical race theory and abortion. Perhaps you identify with proponents of critical race theory or the Black Lives Matter movement. If so, I ask that you read with an open mind and know that I do not consider you an enemy. I am an advocate for truth and life, and I hope that through this conversation, you'll join me.

Perhaps you've had an abortion or supported the abortion industry in some way in the past. I want you to know that God loves you, and because of the price Jesus paid on the cross, He stands ready to forgive you. Life is valuable beyond measure, and that includes yours.

THE BIBLICAL BOOK of 1 Chronicles tells us of a time when men from every tribe of Israel came to David to declare their allegiance after he became king over Israel. The delegation from Issachar is forever lauded in the pages of Scripture as "men who understood the times and knew what Israel should do" (12:23). While the issues have changed, the need for men and women who understand the times has not. That is, in part, why I have written this book.

My hope is that as you read, you'll gain a better understanding of the times in which we find ourselves, and that, by understanding, you'll be better equipped to stand up for what is right. I also hope you'll join me in the ERACED movement to preserve life and love people of every color and race.

A NOTE TO THE READER

I am writing these words in early 2022, after the *Dobbs v. Jackson Women's Health Organization* case was argued in front of the Supreme Court but before a ruling has been handed down. By the time you are reading this, however, the predictions of some legal analysts may have already come true: that the decision from the conservative-majority court will overturn *Roe v. Wade.* If that is the case—and I pray that it is—I want you to know that our fight is not yet over. The content related to abortion in this book still applies.

Roe v. Wade being overturned will not make abortion illegal across the fifty states. Rather, such a decision would simply return the question of abortion back to the state legislatures to decide. It's likely that, very quickly, many red states will pass laws that either outlaw abortion altogether or significantly limit the practice. However, there is no reason to believe that abortion will be curtailed at all in blue states.

The landmark 1973 decision *Roe v. Wade* changed America forever, but the battle for life does not end with the toppling of *Roe*. We must continue to fight for every unborn child, and we cannot rest until the evil of abortion is a thing of the past in every state.

"The plain truth is, within the space of our lifetimes, much of what Americans once almost universally abhorred has been packaged, perfumed, gift-wrapped, and sold to us as though it had great value. By skillfully playing on our deeply felt national values of fairness, generosity, and tolerance, these marketers have persuaded us to embrace as enlightened and noble that which all previous generations since America's founding regarded as grossly self-destructive—in a word, evil."

—David Kupelian

The Marketing of Evil: How Radicals, Elitists, and Pseudo-Experts Sell Us Corruption Disguised As Freedom

CHAPTER 1
KEEP YOUR EYE ON THE BALL

H idden in the losses we experience, there are lessons that shape who we will one day be, but only if we know where to look.

I can't say that I was thinking about important issues like systemic racism, eugenics, or the indoctrination of young children when I walked off the football field at Cardinal Gibbons High School one day in the fall of 2001. Our team had just suffered a humiliating defeat, and my forest green jersey had the grass stains to prove it. Sometimes you're outplayed; other times, you're outsmarted. This was the latter.

Our opponent that day, the Spring Creek Gators, repeatedly broke through our defensive line, but it wasn't because their offense was faster or stronger; it was because they got us to take our eyes off of the ball. At halftime, Coach Troy

Davis berated us. He could see what was happening. "Follow your assignments!" he shouted. "Read the ball!" he thundered, slamming his fist into a steel locker. And whether out of frustration or because he honestly thought we were too dumb to get it the first time, he repeated himself again and again: "Read the ball! Read the ball!"

The Gators were masters of misdirection. Play after play, they divided us, confused us, and outmaneuvered us. They caught us looking away time and time again because we took our eyes off of the one thing that mattered—the ball.

It's never fun to lose, but I learned an invaluable lesson about football that day: disciplined defensive players learn to read the ball. There was a lesson about life to be learned as well: distractions are deadly because they keep a person from seeing the truth.

MISDIRECTION IS a strategy that works equally as well in our culture as it does in football. Of course, you'd have to be paying attention to notice. And that's precisely the problem: so many people are focused on the distractions that they miss what's really happening.

Take, for example, the case of George Floyd. Just reading his name probably brought certain thoughts to your mind: *police brutality, racism, murder.* On May 25, 2020, George Floyd was killed by police officer Derek Chauvin in

Minneapolis, Minnesota. Responding to a call from a store clerk who suspected Floyd might have been passing off counterfeit bills, Chauvin placed Floyd under arrest and in handcuffs. With Floyd restrained and lying face down on the ground, Chauvin placed his knee on Floyd's neck for more than eight solid minutes. Video reveals Floyd said "I can't breathe" more than twenty times[1] and shows that Chauvin did not remove his knee even after Floyd lost consciousness. In fact, it was a full minute and twenty seconds *after* the paramedics arrived that Chauvin finally got up.[2]

It's difficult to watch the video. It's clear that Floyd is suffering. His cries for help go unanswered. Chauvin has his hands in his pockets the entire time. His life is not in danger. There is no compelling reason to use such force.

Whether or not Floyd was guilty of the crime for which he was being arrested, he should not have died in police custody. According to Police Chief Medaria Arrandondo's statements, Officer Chauvin violated the rules of conduct for the Minneapolis Police Department and his actions caused the death of George Floyd. Chauvin was convicted of murder on April 20, 2021. He was later sentenced to serve twenty-two and a half years in prison for his crime.

At the time of Floyd's death, there was little debate about the facts of the case. The whole despicable, awful scene was caught on video and broadcast for all the world to see. Voices from both the Left and the Right condemned

Chauvin's actions and agreed that Floyd's death was a senseless tragedy. But before long, George Floyd became more than a victim; he became the face of systemic racism infecting every aspect of our society. He was turned into an icon to remind us that unchecked police brutality, intimidation, and terror are a daily reality for black Americans, especially young, black men. The chant "I can't breathe" reemerged as a rallying cry at protests and riots alike, the latter of which was deemed legitimate by politicians and mainstream media outlets because, we were told, the country is more racist today than it has been at any other point since the Civil War.

But is all that true? Is there really a nationwide epidemic of white police officers killing unarmed black victims? Is the country really more racist today than it was during the Jim Crow era?

Let's begin by having a look at what the media *didn't* say about George Floyd. Journalists did not think it important to note that Floyd was forcibly resisting arrest and began complaining that he couldn't breathe while still on his feet. In fact, *The New York Times* selectively edited video footage of the arrest showing Floyd struggling against officers' attempt to handcuff him.[3] And, because of an agenda-driven bias for selective reporting—always in an effort to arouse anger and instill fear—few Americans are aware of the state's refusal to relocate the trial or sequester the jury,[4] or allegations of jury intimidation[5] and juror misconduct.[6]

Sadly, this sort of media malfeasance in the service of advancing a leftist agenda is nothing new. In the 1930s, most western reporters colluded with Joseph Stalin to hide his genocidal campaign—estimated to have taken the lives of as many as 10 million—to starve the people of Ukraine. The worst *New York Times* Moscow correspondent Walter Duranty would say about the *Holdomor* (Ukranian for "extermination by famine")[7] was that "the Soviet experiment is not a happy one [but] the suffering inflicted is done with a noble purpose." The Moscow press corps doubled down after journalists like Gareth Jones and Malcolm Muggeridge were able to slip into Ukraine and emerged to tell the real story. Duranty and his colleagues mocked and refuted them with lines like, "conditions are bad, but there is no famine" and "you can't make an omelet without breaking eggs." Duranty's lies "made him one of the most influential journalists of his time." He was awarded a Pulitzer Prize and was invited to the home of then-Governor Franklin Roosevelt. "I asked all the questions this time. It was fascinating." Roosevelt gushed. Russia continues to deny its role in the *Holdomor*, the Pulitzer Committee never rescinded Duranty's award, and Roosevelt went on to impose his own brand of socialism on the United States from the White House.[8]

While the United States isn't a perfect country, the media's unrelenting focus on George Floyd was—and still is —a distraction designed to keep us from seeing what's really going on. And the death of George Floyd is just one example. There are countless other cherry-picked news stories that fit a certain narrative designed to divide us and take our eyes off of what's really important. And while we're all looking the wrong way, a bitter and insidious form of racism is doing more harm to black communities than the police ever could. This racist ideology takes many forms, but two of the most potent and deadly are critical race theory and the abortion rights movement.

Before we dive into those topics, however, I want to highlight a news story that perhaps you didn't hear about. It was reported by certain media outlets, but the murder of David Dorn didn't receive anywhere near the amount of attention paid to the death of George Floyd. That's despite the fact that, like Floyd, Dorn was a black man who was murdered in cold blood.

At seventy-seven years of age, David Dorn was a retired police captain who had served the city of St. Louis courageously for thirty-eight years, but in the early morning hours of June 2, 2020, Dorn was found dead on the sidewalk outside of his friend's pawn shop. He had been there to protect the store from rioters and looters in the wake of the George Floyd killing. When looters approached the store, they shot Dorn in the torso and left him for dead. Stephan Cannon and Mark Jackson, both black, were charged with Dorn's murder.

When the story broke, it was downplayed by certain

segments of the media. On CNN, for example, anchors failed to mention Dorn by name. That evening's coverage even saw then-anchor Chris Cuomo lamenting that the protests would now have a stain upon them. "Now too many see the protests as the problem. No, the problem is what forced your fellow citizens to take to the streets: persistent, poisonous inequities and injustice." He added, "And please, show me where it says protesters are supposed to be polite and peaceful."[9]

Why did one news story about a murdered black man capture the headlines for days and weeks on end while another was brushed aside and bemoaned as a problem? David Dorn was ignored by large swaths of the media precisely because his story does not fit the narrative they'd like to tell. The radical Left, including many in the Democratic Party, want the rest of us to believe there is a race war bubbling underneath the surface in our society, ready to boil over at any minute. They insist a rising tide of white supremacy is the single greatest threat to our nation.

The rallying cry, "Black lives matter!" is difficult to argue with—and who would want to? Of course black lives matter. Only the most vile and detestable of human beings would believe otherwise. But didn't David Dorn's life matter? What about all the black lives taken by other black lives in gang violence? And what about the thousands upon thousands of black babies who are killed in their mother's womb each year? Don't those lives matter?

The Left doesn't want us to ask these questions, so they attempt to distract us with a false narrative. They repeat the same lies over and over again until they sound like truth, all to get us to take our eye off the ball.

I GREW up on the wrong side of the tracks in Raleigh, NC. My mom worked as an assistant in a local nursing home, making just north of twenty-eight thousand dollars a year. We were poor, so everything in our house was rationed. I remember arguing with my brothers and sister at the breakfast table over whose cereal bowl had more milk.

Because money was always tight, life was never easy, but my mom taught me to be positive and put my trust in God, no matter what happened. Once, when we were living in a shelter, sharing what little we received with other families in desperate need, I remember my mom saying, "Thankfully, we don't have a mortgage or rent to pay this month." Now, that's looking on the bright side!

I was in high school when I first heard about a football camp being offered on the campus of North Carolina State University. A camp like that could open doors to scholarships, and I just knew it was the golden ticket I needed. There was only one problem: we barely had enough money to make ends meet (some of the time). Football camp was a luxury we simply couldn't afford. So I decided to pay my own way, and to do so, I launched my first fundraising campaign.

I went door to door, requesting financial assistance from every business in town, but the answer was always no. And then I met Ron Sharpe of JEDCO Construction. Not only did Mr. Ron, as I call him, encourage me, he also picked up the phone to make sure there was a place for me at camp. I was just a poor sixteen-year-old kid and Mr. Ron saw my potential, and he didn't want it to go to waste. A few years later, I was playing football for NCSU under Coach Chuck Amato on a full scholarship.

Because Mr. Ron had taken a chance on me, I decided to give back to my community. I became a youth leader in the city and spent my free time working with troubled kids. The influence of Mr. Ron and my time as a youth leader challenged many of my earlier assumptions. I determined not to paint anyone with a broad brush based on their race or culture. I didn't know it at the time, but the Lord was preparing me for a battle yet to come.

One of the greatest sources of misdirection these days comes from a school of thought known as critical race theory (CRT). A few years ago, CRT was thrust into the public consciousness as if from out of nowhere, but in truth, CRT is nothing new. CRT is a philosophy born out of critical theory, which believes certain social structures exist to dominate and oppress various groups of people while benefitting others. Critical theory is inherently Marxist in its orientation because it views the world through a lens of class warfare. In the case of CRT, the oppressed groups are minority races, especially blacks, who have been the victims of a racist system that has been imposed upon them by the white majority. Everything from punctuality to proper spelling to rewards based on merit are all seen as "white values" designed to keep blacks down.

Part of the problem defining CRT is that its contours are so vague. Law professor Kimberle Crenshaw, one of CRT's progenitors, writes that the theory itself is a verb rather than a noun.

"CRT is not so much an intellectual unit filled with stuff – theories, themes, practices and the like – but one that is dynamically constituted by a series of contestations and convergences pertaining to the ways that racial power is understood and articulated in the post-civil rights era," she said.

She went on to say: "I want to suggest that shifting the frame of CRT toward a dynamic rather than static reference would be a productive means by which we can link CRT's past to the contemporary moment."[10]

In other words, CRT is ever-evolving, changing as new issues related to race and justice arise. This "feature" makes the theory especially difficult to combat. What might have been seen as the stuff of everyday life in society just a few years ago is now explained as racist and products of white privilege.[11]

Critical race theorists do not believe that racism is necessarily and exclusively the product of sinful human hearts. Instead, racism exists primarily in the structures of society. "It is embedded in America's legal system, institutions, and free enterprise system, and imposes 'whiteness' as the societal norm. The system, including capitalism, is 'rigged' to reward white behavior and preserve white supremacy."[12] White people, according to this way of thinking, are inherently racist. It cannot be helped; it's part of their DNA.

The picture painted by proponents of CRT is bleak. If racism is baked into every area of society and every system that pervades our lives, what hope is there? The short answer: there isn't any. The solution, according to many CRT advocates, is to tear down the system completely. Our institutions, laws, free markets, and traditions all have to go. But this won't happen overnight, so to move things along, whites must denounce their "white privilege" to stand in solidarity with blacks. The result is a reversal of Jim Crow, a society where whites are discriminated against, so to speak, and where "separate but equal" means whites are not welcome.

But the answer to racism cannot be more racism, and the remedy for white supremacy, where it does exist, cannot be a new system of black supremacy. Scripture doesn't tell us to repay evil with evil, but to overcome evil with good (1 Peter 3:9). Jesus said, "I tell you, do not resist an evil person. If anyone slaps you on the right cheek, turn to them the other cheek also" (Matthew 5:39). He wasn't telling His followers to be passive and weak. Rather, He was calling them to be strong enough to respond to evil with love.

The deception of CRT is subtle. "Equity" sounds like a good thing, doesn't it? But equity is a far cry from equality. When we talk about equality, we mean things like equal protection under the law or equal opportunities, but equity is a different beast entirely. As then-vice presidential candidate Kamala Harris put it, "Equitable treatment means we all end up in the same place."[13] There was a time where guaranteed outcomes sponsored by the government went by another name: *communism.*

CRT is insidious because while it promises to right wrongs, it does nothing to lift anyone up. White people, of course, are condemned as racist, regardless of their specific actions. They're turned into second-class citizens at best and demonized at worst. But black people are no better off. Individual responsibility is replaced with predetermined outcomes, so blacks are robbed of the dignity that comes with hard work and determination.

Standing in Mr. Ron's office all those years ago, it wasn't white versus black. I didn't ask him for help because he was white, and it wasn't because I was black, (and thus somehow a pawn to assuage his white-guilt) that he aided me. It was much more basic than that. He wanted to help me because he recognized I had the potential to do something great with my life. But it was still up to me. I had to work hard to get noticed. I earned my scholarship to North Carolina State, and it had nothing to do with the color of my skin. I will always be grateful to Mr. Ron, but I can also hold my head up high, knowing I did what needed to be done to change the course of my own life.

Critical race theory threatens to rob young black men and women of similar experiences. When rewards are handed out based on little more than race, it will be difficult to tell the difference between true accomplishments and undeserved handouts. Kindnesses like Mr. Ron's will be obligatory and tainted with lingering questions about motive. Worse than all of that, however, is that critical race theory puts an insurmountable barrier between whites and blacks, even in the church. Instead of learning to see each other as brothers and sisters united together in our love for Christ, we will forever be at odds.

THE OTHER GREAT misdirection of our time is abortion. Like critical race theory, many people in the black community don't see it as a problem. But abortion is, at its core, racist and it destroys more black lives than other single cause of death in the US. There are people on the Left who don't want you to know that. They want you to put on your Black Lives Matter T-shirt and forget all about these black lives—the 19 million black lives that have been ended through abortion since the *Roe v. Wade* ruling in 1973.[14]

Years ago, when my wife, Crystal, and I were expecting our second child, we received some troubling news from the doctor. Crystal was diagnosed with having an ectopic pregnancy, meaning our baby was not growing properly inside Crystal's uterus. Because Crystal's life could be in danger, the recommendation was to terminate the pregnancy. Crystal and I prayed, and we decided not to follow the doctor's advice. We chose, instead, to trust God. Today, our daughter Pamelyn is an honor-roll student in her elementary school who will eat cheese on just about anything except hamburgers.

After our pregnancy scare, we attended a church service in which Bishop Patrick Lane Wooden Sr. shed light on the problem of fatherlessness in the black community, and the devastating impact abortion has had on black families. As I listened, I was thankful that Crystal and I had chosen life, and I realized abortion is just as much an issue for fathers as it is for mothers. I thought about my own daughter, and then I thought about the countless other daughters and sons who have been thrown away (simply because their mothers felt cornered) and believed the lie that abortion was the only way out. I knew I needed to take a more active role in the pro-life movement.

When I visited a local abortion clinic, I encountered twenty different mothers who were there to have an abortion. Fifteen of them were black. I looked around and saw only a few men of color present. Most of the fathers were absent. Everything about the picture I was seeing was terribly wrong.

As I began talking with others about the pro-life cause, I was surprised to find little support in the black community. One person asked me with all sincerity, "Why are you fighting that white man's issue?" I didn't understand. I thought to myself, *How could this be a white man's issue when most of the babies being aborted in this country are black, even though blacks make up just a fraction of the population?* Quite literally, nothing does more harm to the black community than abortion on demand, and yet black men and women overwhelmingly vote for candidates who champion abortion rights.

Abortion clinics, operated primarily by Planned Parenthood, are placed, by and large, in inner-city black neighborhoods. That's not by accident. The founder of Planned Parenthood, Margaret Sanger, considered blacks and other non-whites "human weeds which threaten the blooming of the finest flowers of American civilization."[15] She openly cooperated with the Ku Klux Klan and candidly admitted her goal was to control and even exterminate the black population in the US. The reason abortion clinics are in black communities is because the abortion industry has, since its inception, targeted black babies. It's racist to the core.

So why have black people largely gone along with this terrible evil? In part it's because the mainstream media, liberal politicians, woke preachers, and pro-abortion advocates have convinced many black Americans that being pro-life is a "white" political position to take. The idea that certain issues can belong to one race or another is a misdirection, but it continues to this day. You may recall that in the last election cycle Joe Biden famously said, "If you have a problem figuring out whether you're for me or Trump, then you ain't black."[16] Such a statement is grossly racist, since it implies that all black people think the same way. Sadly, Biden got away with that line, since an overwhelming majority of black voters—92 percent—did indeed vote for the Democratic candidate for president in the 2020 election.[17]

Another reason many blacks ostensibly support pro-abortion policies is that, for decades, the issue of abortion has been entwined with the larger Democratic Party platform. In a two-party system, voters don't have the luxury of picking and choosing national candidates based on specific issues. Rather, voting is often reduced to choosing between two baskets of positions—take them all or leave them all. Since the Left is in favor of large government programs that offer incentives to the poor, most blacks continue to support candidates who push for easy access to abortion in black communities.

POLITICAL COMMENTATORS on the Left are keen to talk about the systemic racism that threatens to destroy our country. In one of the single greatest misdirection plays of our day, they imagine white nationalism is the greatest existential threat to our nation while ignoring the publicly sponsored twin plagues of CRT and abortion. One reaches for our kids in the classroom; the other destroys our children before they leave the womb. Both will destroy America as we know it if left unchecked.

Misdirection is a form of deception, a subtle lie that leads people to think, say, or do something they otherwise wouldn't do. Because of that, good people, many of whom claim to follow Christ, support CRT in schools. It's not because they want to impose a new form of Jim Crow in America. Rather, it's because they believe black people have been treated terribly for much of the history of this country and one way to start to right that wrong is to offer them favored status in many of our nation's vital systems. But as we will see, CRT does not right wrongs; it only creates new ones. Similarly, many otherwise decent people have fallen for the lie that abortion is somehow a mercy for the poor, as sick a thought as that is.

The good news is this: misdirection plays can be spotted, and our defense can adjust. We just have to remember the truth. When it comes to issues of race and equality, Scripture is crystal clear: "There is neither Jew nor Gentile, neither slave nor free, nor is there male and female, for you are all one in Christ Jesus" (Galatians 3:28). The apostle Paul wrote these words to a diverse group of believers in the region of Galatia. He was reminding them that, whatever they were before, their new identity in Christ is more important.

The loudest voices in our culture today want to divide us. They want us to retreat to our tribes and see each other as so different that there's no way we'll ever be able to find common ground. This spirit of *us versus them* is all too real in the church today. As Martin Luther King Jr. noted in 1960, "I think it is one of the tragedies of our nation, one of the shameful tragedies, that eleven o'clock on Sunday morning is one of the most segregated hours, if not the most segregated hour, in Christian America."[18] Sadly, this is still the case in our day. But the truth is, we do have common ground, even if we are too distracted at times to see it. That common ground is the blood-splattered dust of Calvary.

It's because of Jesus' death that we have a future—and by God's grace we'll share that future with people of every tribe, tongue, and nation. Until then, we must keep our eye on the ball and remember our common identity in Christ.

"There is no limit to suffering human beings have been willing to inflict on others, no matter how innocent, no matter how young, and no matter how old. This fact must lead all reasonable human beings, that is, all human beings who take evidence seriously, to draw only one possible conclusion: Human nature is not basically good."

–Dennis Prager

CHAPTER 2
NOTHING NEW UNDER THE SUN

Solomon was the wisest man of his day. Some say he was the wisest person who ever lived. That wouldn't be surprising, given the source of his wisdom.

Shortly after receiving the throne from his father, David, Solomon went to Gibeon to offer sacrifices to God. While he was there, the Lord appeared to him in a dream and said to him, "Ask for whatever you want me to give you" (1 Kings 3:5). It was an unbelievable offer—a virtual blank check from the Creator of the universe. Solomon could have asked for literally anything his heart desired. And what did his heart desire above all else? Wisdom.

Solomon knew God had entrusted him with a sacred task: to lead the people He had chosen out of all the peoples of the world. Israel was God's portion, the children of Abraham through whom the Lord would bless the whole world. Solomon surely felt the weight of the responsibility he had been given, and so he asked God for wisdom. Scripture tells us, "Solomon's wisdom was greater than the wisdom of all the people of the East, and greater than all the wisdom of Egypt. He was wiser than anyone else" (4:30–31). Therefore, we would do well to learn all we can from him. As Proverbs 13:20 advises, "Walk with the wise and become wise."

One of the writings Solomon left to us is the book of Ecclesiastes, a work in which he seeks out nothing less than the meaning of life. Investigating the common trappings in which people seek fulfillment—work, wealth, pleasure—Solomon finds it all to be meaningless. Worse than that, no matter how many decades or centuries or eons humanity "advances" through, it's all been done before. "What has been will be again, what has been done will be done again; there is nothing new under the sun" (1:9). Bleak as that may sound, any student of history knows it to be a true statement.

It may seem like we're living in unprecedented times, but there really is nothing new. In this chapter, we'll consider four current trends connected to critical race theory and abortion—both plagues on our society and bloated forms of racism in action—and we'll see that there really is nothing new under the sun.

∾

IT WAS a warm Wednesday morning in September when nine new students entered Central High School in Little Rock, Arkansas for the first time. Normally, a few new students beginning their studies at a public high school would hardly be noticed. It certainly wouldn't make history. But this was 1957, these nine students were people of color and until that moment, Central High had been an all-white school.

Armed troops from the US Army's 101st Airborne Division escorted Melba Pattillo Beals, Minnijean Brown, Elizabeth Eckford, Ernest Green, Gloria Ray Karlmark, Carlotta Walls LaNier, Thelma Mothershed, Terrence Roberts, and Jefferson Thomas past a mob of angry white students and adults protesting the integration of the school. This was not the nine's first attempt to enter the school and attend classes. The school year had actually begun on September 4, and these black students had tried on several occasions to begin attending Central High, but each time they were met by troops from the Arkansas National Guard, who barred them from crossing the threshold.

Three years had passed since the Supreme Court had declared "separate but equal" unconstitutional in the United States in the famous *Brown v. Board of Education* ruling. But there were many people in the South who refused to comply with the decision. Among them was Arkansas governor Orval Faubus. It was Faubus who ordered the National Guard to block any black students from entering Central High. He claimed it was for their own protection, since violence and bloodshed would be likely if they were allowed to matriculate.

President Eisenhower tried to convince Faubus to remove the National Guard from the school, but Faubus forced the president's hand. Eisenhower sent in twelve hundred federal troops to take charge of the Arkansas National Guard and make sure the Little Rock Nine, as they became known, were permitted entry into the school.

That school year was filled with harassment, intimidation, and, at times, violence for the Little Rock Nine. "Melba Patillo, for instance, was kicked, beaten and had acid thrown in her face. At one point, white students burned a black effigy in a vacant lot across from the school. Gloria Ray was pushed down a flight of stairs, and the Little Rock Nine were barred from participating in extracurricular activities."[1] Ernest Green, the only senior in the group and therefore the first black graduate of Central High, said the year was "like going to war every day."[2]

Racism is an ugly beast with claws that can destroy lives, rip communities apart, and fracture the church. The worst part about this beast is that its hunger is insatiable, and it's impossible to kill. Simply put, racism will not be eradicated until Jesus returns and ushers in a new age. It, like every other manner of sin, emanates from human hearts cursed by the fall. That, of course, doesn't mean we should let the beast of racism run free. We should do everything we can to oppose it, restrain it, and subdue it. At the same time, we should not be surprised that, after all these years, we haven't been able to kill it.

Although the Declaration of Independence states "all men are created equal," the institution of slavery kept this statement from being recognized by the law until after the Civil War. In 1865, the Thirteenth Amendment to the Constitution was ratified, officially ending slavery in the United States. The Fourteenth Amendment, ratified three years later, strengthened the legal rights of newly freed slaves by stating, among other things, that no state shall deprive anyone of either "due process of law" or "equal protection of the law." In reality, though, it would be many decades before due process or equal protection were granted to many black Americans.

Blacks were treated differently than whites in many parts of the country, especially the South. In fact, many states passed laws to legally segregate the races. Such laws decreed that blacks and whites could not use the same restrooms or drinking fountains, ride the same public transportation, or attend the same schools. These laws came to be known as "Jim Crow laws."

There's no equality to be found when people are separated by their skin color, told where they can sit, where they can live, and where they can attend school. Even worse is that a policy of "separate but equal" ensures that people from different races, socio-economic backgrounds, and experiences will never really overcome what divides them. Instead, segregation celebrates the chasm, and both sides lose.

On the one hand, it seems we've come a long way since that bright Wednesday morning when the Little Rock Nine showed the world what composure and grace look like in the face of hostility and systemic oppression. It's hard to imagine such a scene playing out at a high school in the United States today. On the other hand, though, "separate but equal" is alive and well wherever CRT is embraced and its ideas are implemented.

In 2021, Columbia University offered special graduation ceremonies for Native Americans, blacks, Latinos, Asians, and LGBTQ students. These were in addition to a community-wide graduation, but even so, these separate ceremonies have all the flavor of Jim Crow in reverse. The school's website offered the following explanation: "These events provide a more intimate setting for students and guests to gather, incorporate meaningful cultural traditions, and celebrate the specific contributions and achievements of their communities."[3] Rather than the "community" being the student body as a whole, race, sexual preference, and gender identity have become the defining markers of a community.

In 2020, New York University moved to begin offering segregated dormitories for students who identify as black, describing the new housing as a way to create a safe space for students of color.[4] Black student unions are common at many large universities, but in recent years, there have been white student unions formed in response.[5] Sadly, schools like Columbia and NYU are not the only one making such changes. A survey of 173 colleges and universities found that "42 percent offer segregated residences, 46 percent offer segregated orientation programs, and 72 percent host segregated graduation ceremonies."[6] An entire generation is being taught through word and example that the most important thing about another person is their race and who they desire to sleep with.

Of course, many on the Left are quick to dismiss these new "separate but equal" standards on American college and university campuses as nothing like Jim Crow. They note, for example, that this separation is voluntary, not mandatory. Its purpose, they say, is to celebrate a person's unique heritage, not brush it aside. But segregating people by race, even when it is self-segregation, has many disastrous and unforeseen consequences.

One of the first steps toward racial reconciliation is exposure to people of other races and backgrounds. Rubbing shoulders in the same workplaces, restaurants, shops, and churches, it becomes difficult to think of someone with different skin color as completely "other." Ideally, such incidental contact leads to conversations and even friendships. It's difficult to hate someone when you have the opportunity to get to know them. But when life is structured in such a way that you spend your days surrounded by people just like you, there are no opportunities to bridge the gaps between the races. Martin Luther King Jr. famously said, "Love is the only force capable of transforming an enemy into a friend."[7] It's hard to find that love when we don't spend much time together.

In addition, having separate dormitories, common areas, and facilities for blacks sends harmful and dangerous messages. To blacks, the message is: The world outside doesn't understand, like, or want you. You will be treated unfairly at every turn. You cannot afford to trust anyone who doesn't look like you. And to whites, the message is: black people must be altogether different. You will never be able to bridge the chasm of understanding required to have any meaningful sort of relationship, so why bother?

But remember—one of the unspoken goals of CRT is to keep blacks and other minority groups angry. The premise of CRT is that the deck is stacked against them. To mix metaphors, it's baked into the cake, and there's nothing that can be done to fix it. All segregation does is stoke the fires. While it's unlikely we'll see a repeat of the scene played out at Central High School back in September of 1957, proponents of CRT want black Americans to feel that they are hated the same way those nine brave students were that day.

～

In the 1890s, Wilmington, North Carolina, was a unique place on the American landscape. The most populous city in North Carolina, it boasted a thriving import-export business. But what made it truly special was that a majority of its citizens (56 percent) were black. Many of these black Americans were professionals and entrepreneurs, and belonged to the city's thriving middle class. A fair number of the alderman, magistrates, and police officers were black as well. There was even a black-owned newspaper in town.

A bit more than thirty years after the final shots were fired in the Civil War, Wilmington was a shining example of progress for all the world to see. Blacks and whites lived side by side, working together for the prosperity of all. But not everyone was happy about it. White supremacists in Wilmington and throughout North Carolina took aim at the city and sought to "retake" Wilmington for whites.

After a campaign of intimidation throughout the state to rig an election in favor of the Democratic Party, the agitators realized Wilmington would require more than voter intimidation and ballot stuffing to change.

Wilmington's local elections were in the spring rather than the fall, so the biracial constitution of the local government remained in place after the attempted coup. So, on November 10, 1898—two days after the election— Alfred M. Waddell, a former congressman and Confederate general, led thousands of white militiamen and vigilantes through the streets of Wilmington. They turned their guns on black citizens, some of whom returned fire. They hunted down elected officials and forced them to resign. They burned down the *Wilmington Record* (the aforementioned black-owned newspaper). Then they rounded up prominent black citizens and white Republicans, forced them onto a train and told them never to return to Wilmington under the threat of death. Many blacks, especially women and children, fled to nearby swamps and cemeteries, and hid out for three days. In the end, sixty blacks lost their lives in the massacre, and more than 2,100 left the city for good.[8]

For decades, powerful white supremacists controlled the history books, so this story wasn't told to students. When it was, it was changed so that the perpetrators were the heroes and the blacks who lost their lives and their homes became the villains. Not only were the black men and women who lived in Wilmington targeted and terrorized; their pain was brushed aside, and they were demonized in the tales told to future generations—all for the crime of being black.

In the summer of 2020, it wasn't just one city that saw violence and terrorism; it was dozens of towns and cities across the United States. From Louisville to Los Angeles and Staten Island to Seattle, Black Lives Matter took to the streets with the full support of Democratic Party leaders and media personalities to protest the killings of George Floyd, Breonna Taylor, and Ahmaud Arbery. And while some sites saw peaceful protests, fires, looting, and brutality against the police were all too common.

Constant throughout the season of rioting was the chant "Defund the police!" On one level, the rationale was clear. It was the police who had killed George Floyd and Breonna Taylor. On the other hand, defunding the police promises to have the most negative impact on the poorest communities, where criminal elements would essentially go unchecked. Black communities would be disproportionately harmed by such a move. Perhaps that's why from 2020 to 2021, support for defunding the police has fallen sharply, especially among black Americans.[9]

While many of the people who gathered across the country likely did so in the pursuit of justice, the tactics used by those who turned peaceful protests into riots and looting sprees are really no different than those employed against Wilmington in 1898. The goal is exactly the same: intimidation. Rather than winning at the ballot box or in the court of public opinion, a campaign of violence serves to force social change by producing fear in any and who all who might stand against such change. At the same time, the BLM movement perpetuates the false narrative that white supremacy is built into every part of our society, thus stoking anger in many black people as well as many "woke" whites.

In Wilmington, a city where whites and blacks had lived and worked peacefully side by side, agitators got whites to take up arms against their black neighbors and sow chaos in the streets. The result was a city changed through violence and terror. In America today, where blacks and whites have come a long way toward racial reconciliation, agitators got men and women of both races to burn down strip malls and loot electronics stores, to throw bricks at police officers and tear down statues. The result, they hope, will be a nation changed through violence and terror. But that's only if we let them change us.

HAVE you ever wondered how truly despicable ideas gain traction in an otherwise decent society? Evil rarely comes through the front door. Instead, it weaves its way into a nation subtly, disguised in the robes of innocence, slowly making its way past the gatekeepers.

When Adolf Hitler tried to transform Germany, he didn't focus all of his energy on the halls of power. Instead, he looked to the youth of the nation:

> These boys and girls enter our organizations [at] ten years of age, and often for the first time get a little fresh air; after four years of the Young Folk they go on to the Hitler Youth, where we have them for another four years. . . . And even if they are still not complete National Socialists, they go to Labor Service and are smoothed out

there for another six, seven months. . . . And whatever
class consciousness or social status might still be left . . .
the Wehrmacht [armed forces] will take care of that.[10]

Hitler understood that to win the nation, he had to win
the youth. So, from the 1920s onward, the Nazi party spent
enormous energy and plenty of resources targeting the
youngest citizens through reading materials, a propaganda
campaign, youth events, and civic activities. The purpose
was to make it seem as though the Nazi party was really an
extension of the youth culture in Germany so that the two
—Nazism and youthful vitality—were one and the same.

After 1933, the Nazi regime purged the public school
system of teachers deemed to be Jews or to be "politically
unreliable." Most educators, however, remained in their
posts and joined the National Socialist Teachers League.
97% of all public school teachers, some 300,000 persons,
had joined the League by 1936. In fact, teachers joined the
Nazi Party in greater numbers than any other profession.[11]

Schools were essential to the Nazi party's efforts to
reshape the minds of the youth. Certain textbooks were, of
course, removed. New books were introduced that replaced
traditional German values with new ones: obedience to the
state, love for Hitler, and antisemitism. The goal was to
remake the youth, and thereby remake the nation, to be
pro-Nazi and pro-Hitler. This would be done by aban-
doning an education system that taught students *how* to

think in favor of one that simply taught them *what* to think.

In our own country, the takeover of the education system has been a bit more gradual, taking decades rather than years, but the effect is the same: to indoctrinate our children with *what* to think rather than to teach them *how* to think. Take, for example, the newfound emphasis on STEM—science, technology, engineering, and math. There is, of course, nothing wrong with learning these subjects. There's also nothing wrong with education being, in part, preparation for a real-world vocation. But when skills training replaces critical thinking, the result is a population of slaves. At that point, education ceases to be a means of escape for oppressed people and instead becomes a tool of their oppression.

The ancient Greeks knew this, and it was the reason they pioneered liberal arts education:

> In speaking of "liberal" education, we certainly do not mean an education that indoctrinates students in the values of political liberalism, at least not in the most obvious sense of the latter phrase. Rather, we use these words to describe an educational tradition that celebrates and nurtures human freedom.[12]

But since all education cannot be skills training for future jobs, many on the Left have sought to turn the study of traditional liberal arts fare—history and literature most notably—into a means of indoctrinating students with a worldview that serves their agenda. *The 1619 Project* is one such attempt.

First published in *The New York Times Magazine* in August of 2019, *The 1619 Project* seeks to reframe American history around one central issue—racism. The ideas presented in the project have since been introduced into many school curricula. The year 1619 is significant because it was the year the first slave was brought to North America. And so, 1619 should be regarded as the year America, with its original sin of slavery, was founded.

The events of 1776 are less important in the eyes of the project's founders, because, according to them, the Declaration of Independence was just a charade. The "Life, Liberty and the pursuit of Happiness" language was really just a mask to disguise the Founding Fathers' real reason for wanting to break free from England: to keep their slaves. Of course, that's simply not true. "Slavery was not under threat from the British. In fact, Britain didn't free the slaves in its overseas colonies until 1833—57 years later, *after* the Declaration of Independence."[13]

The 1619 Project contends that America's prosperity, even today, can be traced back to the institution of slavery. This claim is also false. All one has to do is consider the relative poverty of the South compared to the North just prior to the Civil War. In every measurable way, the North—without slavery—was much more prosperous than the slaveholding South. Add to that the estimated $5.2 billion spent on the war and the 360,000 Union soldiers who gave their lives to free the slaves, and it is clear slavery was not economically sustainable or advantageous for the United States. American prosperity came *after* the conclusion of the war, not before or because of it.

Perhaps most damaging of all is *The 1619 Project's* insistence that the foundation of America is racism, and since racism is so central to the nation's identity, it's unchangeable. It's part and parcel of who we are. We will always have racism with us, and the soul of America will always be evil. Certainly, the United States is not a perfect country. Our past is spotted with sins and scars, slavery and racism being among the ugliest; but racism does not define America. Wilfred Reilly, associate professor of political science at Kentucky State University, points out, "Today, America is the most successful multi-racial country in history, the only white majority country to elect a black president—twice. . . . To compare American attitudes about race today to America a hundred years ago, let alone to 1619, is absurd." [14]

The 1619 Project is racist at its core. In the picture of America painted by *The Project*, the problems in the black community all stem from slavery and racist institutions at work in this country. In other words, black Americans are victims of a heinous plot. They have been robbed of the American dream—a dream which turned out to be a lie anyway. White people on the other hand, even those who don't descend from slaveowners, are the recipients of stolen prosperity. Once again, whites and blacks are pitted against each other. Students are made to feel they are part of warring tribes, not fellow Americans. There is no space for reconciliation, only blame and bitterness.

What is the purpose of *The 1619 Project*? Proponents of the radical curriculum seek to completely undermine America. If the history of the nation is one constant and unceasing stream of racism and animosity toward minorities, then how can the United States be considered exceptional today? How can American values be viewed as admirable on the world stage when their roots grow in such wretched soil? If America as it exists today can be deemed illegitimate, then the country, as well as its systems, institutions, and values, can be remade. And that is the end goal: to remake America.

THE HEBREWS WERE no threat to the Egyptians, and yet Pharaoh saw them as a great enemy to be destroyed. "The Israelites have become far too numerous for us. Come, we must deal shrewdly with them or they will become even more numerous and, if war breaks out, will join our enemies, fight against us and leave the country" (Exodus

1:9–10). The solution was first to enslave them, and then to slaughter their children.

About a thousand years later, the Hebrews were the target of genocide once again. This time, the world power was Persia:

> Then Haman said to King Xerxes, "There is a certain people dispersed among the peoples in all the provinces of your kingdom who keep themselves separate. Their customs are different from those of all other people, and they do not obey the king's laws; it is not in the king's best interest to tolerate them. If it pleases the king, let a decree be issued to destroy them, and I will give ten thousand talents of silver to the king's administrators for the royal treasury." (Esther 3:8–9)

In both cases, the people of God were blamed for unseen and unrealized trouble. Their persecution was not due to some action on their part but was instead prompted by fears of what could be. *What if they rose up against us? What if they joined our enemies?* Fear is a powerful weapon, gripping the hearts of men and women so they stand idly by while the innocent are slaughtered.

Just in case you thought this type of violence was only an ancient problem, it was the same fear at work in Germany in the 1930s when the Nazis targeted the Jewish people. On January 30, 1939, Adolph Hitler proclaimed:

For hundreds of years Germany was good enough to receive these elements [the Jews], although they possessed nothing except infectious political and physical diseases. What they possess today, they have by a very large extent gained at the cost of the less astute German nation by the most reprehensible manipulations.

Today we are merely paying this people what it deserves....

At the moment, Jews in certain countries may be fomenting hatred under the protection of a press, of the film, of wireless propaganda, of the theater, of literature, etc., all of which they control.[15]

Can you see what Hitler was doing? He was portraying the Jewish residents of Germany as the root cause of the nation's problems. Then he instilled fear in his listeners by supposing that the Jews held all the power. You can almost imagine the murmuring in the crowd: *Someone needs to stand up to the Jews. Someone needs to set Germany free before it's too late.* This fear born from madness resulted in the murder of more than six million Jews before World War II finally ended in 1945.

Today, there is another holocaust of sorts. But this time it's aimed at the black community in the United States. Abortion has taken the lives of more than 19 million black children since the historic *Roe v. Wade* Supreme Court ruling in 1973. To put that in perspective, the population of New York State is roughly 19 million people.[16] According to a report from the Centers for Disease Control and Prevention, abortion disproportionately affects the black community: "[B]lack women make up 14 percent of the childbearing population. Yet, 36 percent of all abortions were obtained by black women. At a ratio of 474 abortions per 1,000 live births, black women have the highest ratio of any group in the country."[17]

In that same report, it was noted, "White women are five times less likely to have an abortion than black women."[18] Why is that? Perhaps it's because "79 percent of Planned Parenthood's surgical abortion facilities are located within walking distance of minority communities."[19] In short, the abortion industry targets the black community, creating an ongoing and insatiable culture of genocide. In the words of Margaret Sanger, the founder of Planned Parenthood, the goal of providing easy access to abortion in black communities was "to exterminate the Negro population."[20]

There is a striking difference between previous attempts at genocide and the extermination of black Americans through abortion. Abortion requires mothers to kill their own children; the black community has been convinced to destroy itself. How? Through the same tactic that is always used: people in power instill fear in those they hope to control. A steady campaign of messages targeting minority women has created a cultural lens through which they view abortion as a key to economic freedom, prolonged health, and sexual freedom.

Abby Johnson, a pro-life advocate and the founder of LoveLine Ministries, used to work for Planned Parenthood as a clinic director, so she saw firsthand how the abortion industry targets vulnerable women. Even though her work was largely behind the scenes, she described being on the team at Planned Parenthood in this way: "You really, unintentionally, become a salesperson for the abortion industry, and you start selling abortions just like you would be selling a car to someone if you worked on a car lot. . . . Women would come in, and even if they were happy about being pregnant . . . then our job became to wreck their plan."[21]

One day on the job, Johnson was asked to come into the operating room, something she didn't normally do. A visiting surgeon was conducting a training exercise and needed an extra pair of hands to hold an ultrasound machine while he performed an abortion. On the screen, Johnson saw with her own eyes an unborn baby fighting against the implement of his own murder. She was disgusted and heartbroken. There was no longer any doubt in her mind that life begins at conception. To her horror, Johnson discovered she was on the wrong side of the fight. A few days later, she tendered her resignation and changed the course of her life. She now tells the world what she saw at Planned Parenthood, and she operates a ministry that aims to help women at every stage of their pregnancy and in their life beyond the birth of their child. In a recent interview, she described the abortion industry in clear detail:

> Planned parenthood and other organizations like them —they are built on killing innocent children, so of course they are that sinister. And you know there's [sic] two reasons: one is because child sacrifice is child sacrifice. Abortion has always been child sacrifice. Human beings have been sacrificing children since biblical times. . . . We just call it something more palatable today. We call it reproductive rights or we call it, you know, women's rights or reproductive justice. But also they're so fervent in their fight for abortion, because it is such a money making industry.[22]

It's no wonder when a terrified black woman goes to the Planned Parenthood location in her neighborhood, she leaves convinced the only way forward is to end the life of her unborn child. The talking points are almost always the same:

- An unwanted child will only make your financial situation worse.
- An unplanned pregnancy will ruin your prospects of meeting someone, settling down, and having the family you've always wanted.

- Having a baby will hinder your career development and put an end to your dreams.
- Black women are more prone to have miscarriages and complications during pregnancy. Abortion is the healthy, responsible choice.

These arguments are lies designed to cover up the beautiful truth: a baby is a precious gift from God, an irreplaceable image-bearer of the Almighty entrusted to their mother and father. Every child has a job to do on this earth: to make it a bit more like heaven. And every child has an eternal destiny: to worship their Creator with every fiber of their being. It's our job as parents and the body of Christ to shepherd them toward this glorious calling.

IN THE NEXT CHAPTER, we'll explore the roots of Planned Parenthood and its targeting of the black community. In so doing, we'll get a clearer understanding of the diabolical schemes at the heart of the abortion industry. But first, I want to take us back to where we began this chapter: in the book of Ecclesiastes.

After exploring every facet of life under the sun, Solomon is no closer to understanding his purpose. "'Meaningless! Meaningless!' says the Teacher. 'Everything is meaningless!'" (12:8). But there is meaning. There is purpose. Solomon needed only to lift up his eyes toward heaven, above the sun. In the eternal realm, where God's will is kept perfectly without the intrusion of sin, there is the answer Solomon was looking for: "Now all has been heard; here is the conclusion of the matter: Fear God and keep his commandments, for this is the duty of all mankind" (v. 13).

History will repeat itself as long we keep living as though there's nothing except what we can see under the sun—that is, if we ignore the God who created us. Like Solomon before us, we must lift up our eyes to heaven and follow the commandments of our Maker. As we walk in His ways, we will find that we can indeed break the cycles of racism, violence, and child sacrifice in our communities. We can start with the twin commandments that Jesus said were the greatest: "'Love the Lord your God with all your heart and with all your soul and with all your mind and with all your strength.' The second is this: 'Love your neighbor as yourself.' There is no commandment greater than these" (Matthew 22:30–31).

It may sound trite, but love really is the answer to many of the evils we face today. Love, grounded in the truth of God's Word and made active through the power of His Spirit, can change the world. Do you believe that?

"Planned Parenthood has repeatedly and excitedly accepted donations earmarked specifically for aborting black babies by callers who stated, 'there are too many blacks,' 'I don't want my kids to face struggles with affirmative action,' and 'the less black people, the better.'

Is there anything wrong with using abortion as a tool of racism, fulfilling Margaret Sanger's dream of less black people?"

–Seth Gruber

CHAPTER 3
MURDER, SHE WROTE

In the Sermon on the Mount, Jesus famously said, "A good tree produces good fruit, and a bad tree produces bad fruit" (Matthew 7:17 NLT). In context, Jesus was warning His disciples and all those listening about false prophets. His point was this: "Just as you can identify a tree by its fruit, so you can identify people by their actions" (v. 20 NLT).

This principle is true not just of trees and prophets but of all people. Sooner or later, a person's actions will tell the world what they're really like. That's why high-profile people who are up to no good will often hire publicists and PR spin doctors to control their narrative. Their evil actions shout the truth to a listening world, but some lackey on retainer is always ready to explain it away or redefine words in order to dupe as many people as possible.

Though Margaret Sanger, the founder of Planned Parenthood, has been dead for more than fifty years, she still has her apologists scrambling to explain away many of the wicked things she said and did. But Sanger's legacy screams too loudly from the streets of inner-city neighborhoods to be ignored. Her despicable beliefs about eugenics, the racial inferiority of non-whites, and a utopian society where the poor and mentally disabled have been eliminated were but seeds that have now grown into a rotten, twisted tree—a blight on Western civilization responsible for the deaths of millions.

FOR YEARS, Planned Parenthood defended Margaret Sanger, claiming that any suggestions she was a racist were simply untrue. They contended that Sanger's associations with eugenicists were just that—associations—but she did not hold to their beliefs. However, in a surprise move in the summer of 2020, Planned Parenthood of Greater New York removed Sanger's name from their flagship clinic in Manhattan, citing "her racist legacy."[1] A short time later, the organization's leadership admitted their detractors had been right about Sanger all along:

> The difficult truth is that Margaret Sanger's racist alliances and belief in eugenics have caused irreparable

damage to the health and lives of Black people, Indigenous people, people of color, people with disabilities, immigrants, and many others. Her alignment with the eugenics movement, rooted in white supremacy, is in direct opposition to our mission and belief that all people should have the right to determine their own future and decide, without coercion or judgement, whether and when to have children.[2]

Removing Sanger's name from a building doesn't remove her beliefs from the DNA of the organization, and denouncing her publicly doesn't change history. It also changes nothing about Planned Parenthood's current operations in this country. All this backpedaling was merely an attempt to control the talking points about racism and abortion after decades of lies failed to hold back the truth. Planned Parenthood now says that Sanger's beliefs don't really matter anyway. The organization isn't racist today, they claim. But the tree Margaret Sanger planted all those years ago is still producing poisonous fruit.

Sanger was a racist, but she wasn't *merely* a racist; she despised all types of people. In a 1932 speech entitled, "My Way to Peace," she described her plan for creating a modern, progressive utopia. "The first step would be to control the intake and output on morons, mental defectives, epileptics."[3] Sanger wanted people living with mental disabilities to be sterilized, to keep from reproducing and multiplying to the next generation the supposed burden they place on society. In fact, the mission statement for The American Birth Control League, Sanger's organization that became the forerunner to Planned Parenthood, was "to promote eugenic birth selection throughout the United States so that there may be more well-born and fewer ill-born children—a stronger, healthier and more intelligent race."[4]

"The second step would be to take an inventory of the second group, such as illiterates, paupers, unemployables, criminals, prostitutes, dope-fiends; classify them in special departments under government medical protection and segregate them on farms and open spaces."[5] Some of these individuals might be permitted back into society, but only if they agreed to be sterilized. Sanger estimated that 15 to 20 million Americans would need to be sterilized or sent to one of her concentration camps. Her vision of a prosperous, new world was one without the poor, the disabled, or those grappling with substance abuse problems—not because she desired to improve the plight of such people but because she wanted them removed from society permanently through any means necessary.

In her book *The Pivot of Civilization*, Sanger wrote,

Eugenics suggests the reestablishment of the balance between the 'fit' and the 'unfit.' The birth-rate among the . . . finer stocks of humanity is to be increased by awakening among the 'fit' the realization of the dangers of a lessened birth-rate in proportion to the reckless breeding of the 'unfit.'[6]

Sanger was so committed to the idea of weeding out the weak and poor, she actually argued against charity: "We are now in a state where our charities, our compensation acts, our pensions, hospitals, and even our drainage and sanitary equipment all tend to keep alive the sickly and the weak, who are allowed to propagate and in turn produce a race of degenerates."[7]

From 1917 to 1940, Sanger published and edited the *Birth Control Review*. On the masthead of every issue was the phrase "Birth Control: To Create a Race of Thoroughbreds."[8] The focus of the magazine was to promote voluntary birth control and eugenics. Among its contributors was Ernst Rudin, Adolf Hitler's Director of Genetic Sterilization and founder of the Nazi Society for Racial Hygiene. It has been demonstrated that Hitler himself read American eugenics literature and formulated his ideas about a master Aryan race from what he perused.[9] Though there is no direct evidence that Hitler read Sanger's *Birth Control Review* specifically, it's not difficult to imagine. Another contributor to Sanger's journal, Julian Sorell Huxley, was the president of the English Eugenics Society and the founder of the World Wildlife Federation. Huxley was undeniably racist, once writing:

The negro mind is as different from the white mind as the negro from the white body. The typical negro servant, for instance, is wonderful with children, for the reason that she really enjoys doing the things that children do. . . . You have only to go to a nigger camp-meeting to see the African mind in operation—the shrieks, the dancing and yelling and sweating, the surrender to the most violent emotion, the ecstatic blending of the soul of the Congo with the practice of the Salvation Army . . . [intermarriage between the] negro and Caucasian type . . . gives rise to all sorts of disharmonious organisms. . . . The American negro is making trouble because of the American white blood that is in him.[10]

While Sanger herself wasn't a card-carrying Nazi and didn't specifically write the detestable things about black people that Huxley did, she was the editor of *The Birth Control Review* during its entire run, making all editorial decisions regarding content and contributors. These associations were not incidental or accidental. She shared her platform with these men because she shared their ideals.

It's important to know that Sanger was a full-throated believer in eugenics. It's key to understanding that her racism, which we'll explore shortly, was not simply due to ignorance or some socially-conditioned prejudice. Deep within Sanger's twisted heart was the belief that human beings are nothing more than animals—free to be sterilized, put out to pasture, or slaughtered in order to improve the lot of those she considered to be the finer specimens in the herd. This wasn't just an error in judgment; it was an attempt to twist the natural order of creation itself.

When it came to birth control—a term she coined—Sanger believed that in the large majority of cases, especially among the poor, large families were a burden to be avoided or eradicated. Early on, she handed out flyers advertising her Brooklyn clinic. In English, Yiddish, and Italian, they read, "Mothers! Can you afford to have a large family? Do you want any more children? If not, why do you have them?"[11] The year was 1916, and though she was not yet providing abortions, it's clear she didn't see children as a blessing but as a weight to be cast off.

SANGER BELIEVED society could be made better if those deemed "undesirable" were walled off or eliminated entirely. She also viewed children as a drain on their parents, and by extension, on their communities. In time she found a way to fuse these twin diabolical beliefs: she brought abortion to black neighborhoods across America.

In a letter to Dr. C. J. Gamble, dated December 10, 1939, about "the Negro Project," she wrote:

It seems to me from my experience where I have been in

North Carolina, Georgia, Tennessee and Texas, that while the colored Negroes have great respect for white doctors they can get closer to their own members and more or less lay their cards on the table which means their ignorance, superstitions and doubts. They do not do this with the white people and if we can train the Negro doctor at the Clinic he can go among them with enthusiasm and with knowledge, which, I believe, will have far-reaching results among the colored people. His work in my opinion should be entirely with the Negro profession and the nurses, hospital, social workers, as well as the County's white doctors. His success will depend upon his personality and his training by us.[12]

Her plan, in bringing abortion clinics into black communities, was to employ black physicians and nurses in order to gain the trust of black mothers. While some people have defended this plan, saying it was actually a very forward-thinking idea, since blacks in the South would likely encounter racism at a predominantly white clinic. However, the emphasis in this letter is not on helping black Americans circumvent the racist tendencies of their white neighbors; rather, it was on convincing them that abortion was the answer to their problems. Sanger also hoped to employ black ministers in her propaganda campaign:

The ministers [sic] work is also important and also he

should be trained, perhaps by the Federation as to our ideals and the goal that we hope to reach. We do not want word to go out that we want to exterminate the Negro population and the minister is the man who can straighten out that idea if it ever occurs to any of their more rebellious members.[13]

That last bit is perhaps the most damning. Sanger admits that her goal is to "exterminate the Negro population." Representatives from Planned Parenthood and fans of Sanger are quick to point out that she merely said she didn't want the idea of black genocide to get out, not that she was hoping to exterminate blacks. However, if that were the case, there would have been no need to label independent-minded blacks as "rebellious." (That's a racist thought in and of itself—that all black people think the same way, and if any deviate, they're out of line or "rebellious.") Here is one critic's worthwhile take on this explosive passage and those who still choose to defend Sanger:

Many who have long studied her believe that she meant those words "to exterminate" as describing a plan she had. However, some mysteriously say she did not mean it that way when she spoke the word "exterminate." At the very least it is highly suspect as to why she would ever choose a word like "exterminate" for communicating what was on her mind about a whole race of people for any reason! It seems to her pro-abortion cohorts that no speech is off limits, and every horrid sounding blurb was just an accidental gaffe, no matter how incredulous, extremely racist and hateful it sounds.[14]

Taken in context, it's clear Sanger hoped to use black physicians and ministers to set minds at ease so no one would realize her intention was population control. Pastors, especially, would help convince black mothers that abortion was the healthy, smart, and financially savvy thing to do. And it wasn't the first time she tried to employ such a tactic.

Ten years before the advent of the Negro Project, Sanger opened an abortion clinic in Harlem, New York, precisely because of the city's large black population. Poverty was a serious problem, and Sanger did everything she could to convince the community that birth control, including abortion, was the solution to the predicament.

Sanger shrewdly used the influence of prominent blacks to reach the masses with this message. She invited [Dr. W. E. Burghardt] DuBois [one of the nation's most influential African Americans and one of the founders of the NAACP] and a host of Harlem's leading blacks, including physicians, social workers, ministers, and journalists, to form an advisory council to help direct the clinic so that our work in birth control will be a constructive force in the community. She knew the importance of having black professionals on the advisory board and in the clinic; she knew blacks would instinctively suspect whites of wanting to decrease their numbers. She would later use this knowledge to implement the Negro Project.

Sanger convinced the community so well that Harlem's largest black church, the Abyssinian Baptist Church, held a mass meeting featuring Sanger as the speaker.[15]

Before long, many in the community came to believe that their cyclical poverty and the problems that came along with it were due, in large part, to the frequency with which children were born. Proponents of Sanger's approach to birth control and abortion argued "birth control was necessary to regulate births in proportion to the family's income; spacing births would help mothers recover physically and fathers financially; physically strong and mentally sound babies would result; and incidences of communicable diseases would decrease."[16]

Gaining a foothold, the propaganda only continued— and spread far beyond Harlem. In 1932, three years after the Harlem clinic opened, Sanger invited a number of black writers to contribute to a special issue of the *Birth Control Review*. The editorial was framed around a single question, designed to get to the heart of Sanger's sales pitch to the black community:

Shall they go in for quantity or quality in children? Shall they bring children into the world to enrich the undertakers, the physicians, and furnish work for social workers and jailers, or shall they produce children who are going to be an asset to the group and American society? The answer: Most [blacks], especially women, would choose quality ... if they only knew how.[17]

Sadly, Sanger's efforts were largely successful. While not everyone bought into birth control and abortion as the answer to the problem of poverty, many did. The pastors of black churches no longer invited Sanger to speak so that she could present her ideas as an option to consider; now, they wanted her there to champion those ideas as the solution to the plight of their flocks. Prominent black newspapers featured Sanger's writings as well.

Rather than attacking the root causes of maternal and infant deaths, diseases, poverty, unemployment, and a host of other social ills, not the least of which was racism, Sanger pushed birth control. To many, it was better for blacks not to be born rather than endure such a harsh existence.[18]

ABORTION HAS BECOME a part of mainstream black culture across America, even in the church. The lies propagated by Margaret Sanger nearly a hundred years ago are still doing damage to the hearts and minds of God's people today. Sanger used the black ministers of her day to gain a foothold in black communities. As a pastor, I feel a special burden to expose Sanger's lies to the truth of God's Word.

Sanger believed there were some people who were fit to live and reproduce, and others who were unfit. But nothing could be further from the truth. When God made the first humans, He made them in His own image (Genesis 1:27). Adam and Eve and all who came after them—you and I included—bear God's likeness. We are not mere animals, as Sanger believed. We were made to be members of God's household and to live forever in His presence. Our status as God's image-bearers is not revoked through poverty, addiction, disease, disability, or race. Every single person is incredibly precious in God's sight. For this reason, it's not an exaggeration to consider Sanger's views on the sanctity of life—and the enduring work of Planned Parenthood—Satanic, for they strike at the very image of God.

And of course, Scripture never views children as a burden. Sons and daughters are a gift to be cherished. "Children are a heritage from the LORD, offspring a reward from him" (Psalm 127:3). Jesus Himself welcomed small children (Luke 18:16), warned those who might cause them to stumble (Matthew 18:6), and said the kingdom of heaven belonged to people who were just like them (19:14). Once again, Sanger is completely out of step with the natural order of creation and the heart of God. If we say we follow the Lord, we cannot tolerate the plague of abortion in our communities.

Scripture gives us this mandate: "Do not conform to the pattern of this world, but be transformed by the renewing of your mind" (Romans 12:2). In other words, we are to push aside the wicked ideas this world presses upon us and replace them with the truth of God's Word. Planned Parenthood tells black mothers and fathers a child is inconvenient, expensive, and a burden to carry. To borrow from King David, the view from the womb—and from heaven—is entirely different:

> *For you created my inmost being;*
> *you knit me together in my mother's womb.*
> *I praise you because I am fearfully and*
> *   wonderfully made;*
> *your works are wonderful,*
> *I know that full well.*
> *My frame was not hidden from you*
> *when I was made in the secret place,*
> *when I was woven together in the depths of the*
> *   earth. (Psalm 139:13–15)*

"Pastors, I beg you to consider what I have written here. I believe the Church—your church—is under attack. As shepherds, we must defend the sheep. We must repel the wolves. And yes, the wolves are many. However, this one is within the gates and has the worst of intentions. He desires to use your genuine love for the brethren as leverage.

Don't let him! Recognize the difference between the voice of the Good Shepherd who calls you to love all the sheep and the voice of the enemy that tells you some of them are guilty, blind, ignorant oppressors and that others are oppressed—all based on their melanin.

Reject cries that take principles and stories of individual restitution (Numbers 5:7; Luke 19) and eisegetically twist them into calls for multi-generational reparations. Reject the cries of those who twist the repentance of Daniel and Ezra 1) on behalf of theocratic Israel and 2) for sin that took place during their lifetime, in an effort to promote multi-generational, ethnic guilt that rests upon all white people by virtue of their whiteness."

—Voddie T. Baucham Jr.

Fault Lines: The Social Justice Movement and
  Evangelicalism's Looming Catastrophe

CHAPTER 4
THE ROLE OF THE BLACK MINISTER

Moses was born to be the deliverer of God's people. Though his beginnings were humble, it was soon clear he was being set apart by the Lord for a special role. While still a baby, Moses was saved from Pharaoh's wicked edict when his mother, Jochebed, placed him in a basket and set him adrift on the Nile River. He was then found by Pharaoh's daughter, who gave him the privilege of growing up in Pharaoh's household. As a result, he received the finest education in the world—plus military training reserved for a select few.

Years later, when God called to Moses from a burning bush on Mount Sinai, Moses was a unique specimen, a shepherd-warrior cultivated and groomed to be a great leader. Even though he had his own personal doubts about the mission God laid before him (see Exodus 3:11–4:17), on paper he was the right man for the job. And yet, being a deliverer takes more than a certain set of skills or a wealth of knowledge—or even the power of God. To be an effective deliverer, the people you're leading have to *want* to be delivered. In the case of God's people, though their feet took them away from Egypt, their hearts never really left. That's one of the reasons God waited for that first generation of Israelites to die off in the wilderness before He permitted their children to enter the Promised Land.

We Americans are not enslaved to a foreign power, but like those early Israelites, we need deliverance. We need rescue from the power of sin. We need freedom from the bondage of dark, spiritual forces. We need victory over the power of death. That's why Jesus came. He is our ultimate Deliverer, the better Moses who leads His people out of slavery, through the wilderness, and into the promised land.

When we put our trust in Jesus Christ, we apply His blood to our lives, not unlike the Hebrew people applying the blood of Passover lambs to their doorframes back in the book of Exodus (see Exodus 12:21–23). We are saved by Jesus' death and come to faith through the power of the gospel. The apostle Paul wrote, "It is for freedom that Christ has set us free. Stand firm, then, and do not let yourselves be burdened again by a yoke of slavery" (Galatians 5:1). Many believers today discover freedom in Christ and initially follow the Lord with all joy, only to lapse after a time and begin pining for "the good ol' days." They want to wallow in their old patterns of sin. They want to be conformed to this world rather than transformed for the kingdom. They are the spiritual descendants of the Israelites who didn't want to be delivered from their slavery, at least not completely. They complained to Moses and Aaron, "If only we had died by the LORD's hand in Egypt! There we sat around pots of meat and ate all the food we wanted, but you have brought us out into this desert to starve this entire assembly to death" (Exodus 16:3).

Though we tend to think of Moses' professional preparation having come from his time in Pharaoh's court, I don't think the forty years Moses spent as a shepherd in Midian were wasted. Just like his education and his military training, the skills he learned as a shepherd shaped him into the leader he would become. God knew that His people were as stubborn as—nay, more stubborn than—sheep. To shepherd God's people, Moses had to be patient and tenderhearted but also unwavering in his guidance. He needed to develop a sixth sense for danger, and he needed to learn what it means to sacrifice his own comfort for the wellbeing of the sheep in his care.

Pastors have been called to lead their churches as a shepherd leads his flock. In that sense, they are to be deliverers like Moses. That is why they must never stop preaching the good news of Jesus Christ, and they must never stop applying the gospel message to every part of life. For it is the gospel that brings deliverance. It is the gospel that releases people from their old sins and the snares of this world. It is the gospel that sets people free.

Of course, we know that the true Deliverer is Jesus, but pastors are His under-shepherds. Peter described the situation this way:

> Be shepherds of God's flock that is under your care, watching over them—not because you must, but because you are willing, as God wants you to be; not pursuing dishonest gain, but eager to serve; not lording it over those entrusted to you, but being examples to the flock. And when the Chief Shepherd appears, you will receive the crown of glory that will never fade away. (1 Peter 5:2–4)

The word *pastor* means "shepherd." It's a powerful image when you stop and think about it. Without a shepherd, the sheep are doomed. They're likely to wander away from the flock and get lost or hurt, and they'll be an easy target for predators. The shepherd is there to keep them alive—to keep them from doing something stupid or getting picked off by critters with sharp teeth.

The pastor's job is to care for his flock, and yet many

pastors don't want to preach the whole gospel. They don't want to teach the whole counsel of God. They are so consumed with keeping the sheep comfortable, they have neglected to prepare them for the dangers they will face in this world. Today, pastors in the West have more training than ever before. There are more books, conferences, classes, and degrees available to ministers, and yet none of it does any good if they do not take hold of the mission God has given them—to lead His people out of bondage.

IN THE LAST CHAPTER, we looked at the philosophy of Margaret Sanger, the founder of Planned Parenthood. When I was first investigating Sanger, one of the things that shocked me was the willingness of pastors to go along with her schemes. Though she was bringing abortion clinics into black neighborhoods in order to—in her own words—"exterminate the Negro population," black ministers allowed themselves to be used as pawns in her evil plan.

And it's not only the issue of abortion that has black pastors endangering the flocks God has put in their care. Progressivism has no shortage of tools and propaganda designed to destroy the lives of the vulnerable and afraid. One of the favorite ploys of the Left as of late is critical race theory. But regardless of the specific issue, the natural question we should be asking is, *Why?* Why would black ministers not do everything in their power to warn the people in the pews about this predator called progressivism that is out to devour them?

Jesse Jackson is one of the most famous black ministers in the US. He is known today for his left-wing politics and his cozy relationship with the Democratic Party. He is also the founder and president of the civil rights organization, the Rainbow PUSH Coalition. Jackson has been very vocal in his support of abortion. For example, in 2021, he decried the "Texas Taliban wing of the Republican Party"[1] on account of a Texas law that restricted abortions when a heartbeat can be detected. But this wasn't always the case. In fact, early in his career and ministry, Jackson was outspoken in his pro-life views:

> The question of abortion confronts me in several different ways. First, although I do not profess to be a biologist, I have studied biology and know something about life from the point of view of the natural sciences. Second, I am a minister of the Gospel and therefore, feel that abortion has a religious and moral dimension that I must consider.
>
> Third, I was born out of wedlock (and against the advice that my mother received from her doctor) and therefore

abortion is a personal issue for me. From my perspective, human life is the highest good, the *summum bonum*. Human life itself is the highest human good and God is the supreme good because He is the giver of life. That is my philosophy. Everything I do proceeds from that religious and philosophical premise.[2]

So what happened to Reverend Jackson to change his mind so dramatically—to go from the belief that life is "the highest good" to viewing pro-life advocates as equivalent to the Taliban? The shift took place in 1988 when Jackson decided to throw his hat in the ring and run for president of the United States. Seemingly out of the blue, he stopped talking about the value of life as it relates to the unborn. He became a proponent for federal funding for abortion. He even went so far as to say moral opinions should have no weight on public policy.[3] Hoping to win the presidency, Jackson fell in line is a loyal soldier in the Democratic Party, the party of abortion, prompting one journalist at the time to remark, "No other candidate this season, fallen or still standing, has shifted positions as radically as Jackson on abortion."[4]

Jackson was ultimately unsuccessful in his quest for the presidency, but seeing the traction he had gained with liberals and progressives on the campaign trail, he stuck with his radical pro-choice stance. He's not alone. Many black pastors in this country are either publicly pro-choice or are silent on the issue of abortion. And while not many of them have tasted fame and fortune the way Jackson has, many have fallen for the same temptation in a different form.

Two thousand years ago, the apostle Paul told his protégé Timothy, "For the time will come when people will not put up with sound doctrine. Instead, to suit their own desires, they will gather around them a great number of teachers to say what their itching ears want to hear" (2 Timothy 4:3). While this description could be applied to many times and places, it is certainly true of our own day. We live in a society in which many people refuse to sit under preaching that makes them uncomfortable. As a result, there are plenty of pastors ready to tailor their messages to the felt needs of their audience rather than their true needs as defined by the gospel.

Because abortion has been culturally acceptable in black churches for decades, it would take a brave minister to speak out against it. Such a message would offend those who lean to the Left politically, those who have had abortions, and those who have shown public support for pro-abortion policies and candidates. In other words, it would be very unpopular in the current climate. However the job of a pastor—the job of a shepherd and deliverer—is not to make sure everyone is comfortable; it's to preach the truth, no matter how uncomfortable it makes certain people, so that men and women might be set free.

The same logic applies to issues stemming from the adoption of critical race theory. Many blacks see CRT as a good thing, simply because the theory claims to be "anti-racist" and to promote the welfare of minority groups in the US. In life under CRT, systemic racism is supposedly challenged and upended, bringing justice and opportunity to black Americans and other historically oppressed communities. It's no wonder it's popular—at least in theory—among a large segment of the black population. But like abortion, it's built on a lie, and it runs counter to the gospel.

Rather than being the sort of pastors that Paul warned Timothy about—those who tickle itching ears—black ministers in this country must strive to be shepherds who take seriously these other words from Paul to his son in the faith: "All Scripture is God-breathed and is useful for teaching, rebuking, correcting and training in righteousness, so that the servant of God may be thoroughly equipped for every good work" (2 Timothy 3:16–17). There are three essential elements in this statement from Paul. Let's consider them one at a time:

1. **All Scripture is God-breathed** . . . We're not talking about just some of the Bible or certain passages or the red letters. *All* of it is breathed out by God. It's all essential, more valuable than the most precious jewels. No verse can be set aside, ignored, or rejected. It's all the Word of the

Lord, and it's all for us, His people. We cannot afford to follow a partial Bible, and pastors cannot properly shepherd God's people by only preaching some of the Scriptures.

2. **. . . and is useful for teaching, rebuking, correcting and training in righteousness . . .** Many people think the point of the Sunday sermon is mere encouragement. They believe they should read their Bible to get a jolt of inspiration or to grow in their knowledge of God and His ways. While the counsel of God certainly does much to encourage, inspire, and inform, it is also meant to teach, rebuke, correct, and train.

3. Many people today are uncomfortable with the idea of being rebuked or corrected by a spiritual authority. In fact, it's common for people to leave a church at the first sign of discipline. That's why many pastors have stopped preaching or teaching anything that might come across as a rebuke or a correction. But this is not God's design for His flock.

4. **. . . so that the servant of God may be thoroughly equipped for every good work.** This is the point of it all. Shepherds are to preach and teach the entire Bible—all Scripture —because it leads to transformed lives that go

out into the world and do good works, making
our communities a bit more like God's kingdom.

Can you see the connection between the loss of gospel
preaching in our churches and the widespread acceptance
of abortion and the explosion of CRT? When pastors
neglect the Scriptures, false teaching thrives. I am singling
out black ministers here, not because white pastors don't
have their own blind spots (we'll get to some of those in the
next chapter) but because CRT and abortion have gained a
foothold in black and minority communities in large
measure because of what's *not* being said from the pulpit in
black churches.

THINKING BACK to the ministry of Moses in the wilderness, it
strikes me that he was unpopular with the people he was
called to lead. The Israelites routinely grumbled against his
leadership. They blamed Moses for their struggles, and they
openly rebelled on occasion. And yet, pleasing the people
was not Moses' aim. Instead, he was concerned with one
opinion and one opinion only: God's. I am convinced that
this attitude cultivated by Moses is the only one a minister
of the gospel should have. Pastors serve God's people by
serving Jesus Christ.

So what does the whole counsel of God tell us about the

issue of abortion? From Genesis to Revelation, the message
of God is a message of life. Death is the enemy. In fact, the
New Testament tells us, "The last enemy to be destroyed is
death" (1 Corinthians 15:26). But from the beginning, the
taking of a life is serious business.

When Cain killed his brother Abel, God said to Cain,
"What have you done? Listen! Your brother's blood cries out
to me from the ground" (Genesis 4:10). Life and death are
nothing to be taken lightly. Human beings are God's image-
bearers, and as such, the penalty for taking a life is severe:
"Whoever sheds human blood, by humans shall their blood
be shed; for in the image of God has God made mankind"
(9:6).

The Bible makes no distinction between the born and
the unborn. Both are precious in the Lord's sight. Just
consider what God said to the prophet Jeremiah: "Before I
formed you in the womb I knew you, before you were born
I set you apart; I appointed you as a prophet to the nations"
(Jeremiah 1:5). Or consider how the unborn John the Baptist
reacted to the sound of Mary's voice: "When Elizabeth
heard Mary's greeting, the baby leaped in her womb" (Luke
2:41). Neither Jeremiah nor John are seen as less than fully
human, less than 100-percent image-bearers of God.

With these Scripture passages in mind, how could
anyone conclude that abortion is an acceptable practice? In
order to condone or champion abortion, these verses have
to be ignored, explained away, or mythologized. But to do

any of those things is to butcher the Word of God. As followers of Jesus, we don't get to decide what parts of Scripture we want to believe and internalize. We are to gratefully receive the entire Bible.

What about critical race theory? Does the Word of God tell us how we should think about CRT? While CRT is a product of twentieth-century Marxist thought, it's not a new philosophy. There were many in the ancient world who thought a person's identity and value should be tied to social status, race, or nationality. But the Bible declares something radically different.

Our value as human beings comes not from some external or superficial characteristic. Rather, it comes from being created by God. Think about this for a minute: God is infinitely powerful, infinitely creative, and infinitely wise. With infinite possibilities stretched out in His imagination, He chose to create you and me and all the people we will meet in our lifetimes. Every one of them, and every person who has ever lived or will lived, is incredibly precious to the Lord. And yet, critical race theory wants to divide us up according to race so that we can lord it over one another.

In the New Testament, another precious truth is added: our identity—no matter where we come from, what color our skin may be, or who our parents are—is found in Jesus Christ. It's a message repeated again and again by the apostle Paul:

For there is no difference between Jew and Gentile—the same Lord is Lord of all and richly blesses all who call on him, for, "Everyone who calls on the name of the Lord will be saved." (Romans 10:12–13)

For we were all baptized by one Spirit so as to form one body—whether Jews or Gentiles, slave or free—and we were all given the one Spirit to drink. (1 Corinthians 12:13)

There is neither Jew nor Gentile, neither slave nor free, nor is there male and female, for you are all one in Christ Jesus. (Galatians 3:28)

Here there is no Gentile or Jew, circumcised or uncircumcised, barbarian, Scythian, slave or free, but Christ is all, and is in all. (Colossians 3:11)

In addition, the New Testament does not teach that the answer to injustice should be more injustice, just aimed in the opposite direction. But that's precisely what proponents of CRT advocate. The new society they imagine sees white people at the bottom, permitted to exist but only with ongoing repentance for the sin of having been born white. Meanwhile, blacks and other minorities get special privileges. In essence, it's racism turned and aimed at those who have benefited from racism in the past. Scripture, however, teaches that our response to evil should never be more evil:

Do not repay anyone evil for evil. Be careful to do what is right in the eyes of everyone. If it is possible, as far as it depends on you, live at peace with everyone. Do not take revenge, my dear friends, but leave room for God's wrath, for it is written: "It is mine to avenge; I will repay," says the Lord. On the contrary:

"If your enemy is hungry, feed him;
   if he is thirsty, give him something to drink.
   In doing this, you will heap burning coals on his head."

Do not be overcome by evil, but overcome evil with good. (Romans 12:17–21)

When Peter asked Jesus how many times he should forgive, the Lord responded, "I tell you, not seven times, but seventy-seven times" (Matthew 18:22). As many commentators have noted, the point here is not that revenge is a viable option after the seventy-eighth transgression. Rather, "Jesus tells Peter and the rest of His disciples that they should forgive continuously and without limit, just as God forgives them. The lavish nature of divine forgiveness requires the same response in human relationships."[5] The Christian life is a life of forgiveness precisely because we have been given life through the forgiveness of God.

~

JESUS KNEW what it was like to preach an unpopular message. He once told a crowd of people, "Very truly I tell you, unless you eat the flesh of the Son of Man and drink his blood, you have no life in you. Whoever eats my flesh and drinks my blood has eternal life, and I will raise them up at the last day" (John 6:53–54). It was a strange teaching, this business of eating the Lord's flesh and drinking His blood. It must have made people question His sanity. Perhaps others were disgusted at the image, not pausing long enough to consider what it even meant. Even His disciples commented, "This is a hard teaching. Who can accept it?" (v. 60).

From that point on, many people stopped following Jesus. They simply walked away because they could not wrap their heads around his preaching—or perhaps they didn't want to. Jesus turned to His disciples and asked, "You do not want to leave too, do you?" (v. 67). I love Peter's response to this question. He leaned in and spoke for the group: "Lord, to whom shall we go? You have the words of eternal life" (v. 68).

As a black minister, I recognize that not everyone in the pews wants to hear the message God has given me to preach. But I will continue to preach it all the same. I will continue to preach the whole counsel of God, the entire message of the Bible—without cherry-picking stories and passages that are easy on the ears. I will continue to encourage people, and I will continue to make people uncomfortable, because it is often in our moments of discomfort that God sets us free.

Scripture contains the very words of God—the words of eternal life. If we reject the Bible, where else can we go?

"The gospel is preached in the ears of all men; it only comes with power to some. The power that is in the gospel does not lie in the eloquence of the preacher otherwise men would be converters of souls. Nor does it lie in the preacher's learning; otherwise it could consists of the wisdom of men. We might preach till our tongues rotted, till we should exhaust our lungs and die, but never a soul would be converted unless there were mysterious power going with it – the Holy Ghost changing the will of man. O Sirs! We might as well preach to stone walls as preach to humanity unless the Holy Ghost be with the word, to give it power to convert the soul."

—Charles Spurgeon

CHAPTER 5

THE ROLE OF THE WHITE
MINISTER

At the close of the last chapter, I mentioned Peter's declaration to Jesus: "Lord, to whom shall we go? You have the words of eternal life" (John 6:68).

Peter, for all his faults, could be very perceptive. He knew Jesus spoke the words of life. He knew that since he was a sinner, he should not be able to stand in Jesus' presence (Luke 5:8).

He also recognized Jesus as "the Messiah, the Son of the living God" (Matthew 16:16). But for all of Simon Peter's perceptiveness, he had some blind spots he was unaware of.

For one, Peter was a bit of a people pleaser. He liked to fit in, to go with the flow. At times, he was afraid of what others might think if he did something they deemed socially unacceptable. The apostle Paul recorded such an incident:

> When Cephas [Peter] came to Antioch, I opposed him to
> his face, because he stood condemned. For before certain
> men came from James, he used to eat with the Gentiles.
> But when they arrived, he began to draw back and
> separate himself from the Gentiles because he was afraid
> of those who belonged to the circumcision group. The
> other Jews joined him in his hypocrisy, so that by their
> hypocrisy even Barnabas was led astray. (Galatians
> 2:11–13)

God had shown Peter that He accepts all people, regardless of their race and apart from the laws of Israel. Back in Acts 10, Peter witnessed Cornelius and his entire household respond to the gospel message and put their faith in Jesus. He watched as these Gentiles were filled with the Holy Spirit and spoke in tongues. If any Jewish Christian knew for certain that God had made a way for Gentiles to enter into the family of God, it was Peter. And yet, when the social pressure was on, he refused to eat with his Gentile brothers and sisters in Antioch.

Peter is not alone. At times, we are all tempted to take the path of least resistance, to give in to the fear of what others might think. However, in doing so, we run the risk of denying the very gospel we are supposed to walk in. That's what happened to Peter. His actions announced to the world that in his heart he wasn't quite ready to accept Gentile Christians into the fold. His refusal to share a meal with Syrians and Greeks shouted loudly that he believed, as a Jew, he was somehow superior.

This chapter is written with white ministers of the gospel in mind, in the hope that being reminded of the whole counsel of God on issues of race and community might help some discover their blind spots. These words are given not to condemn or to blame but to gently correct and to encourage. I do not believe that most white Christians knowingly and intentionally do or say things to hurt their black brothers and sisters, and so I trust that my words will be received in the spirit in which they are offered.

IN THE SUMMER OF 2020, Black Lives Matter protestors were all over the news, marching through cities, often destroying property along the way. The images are disturbing, but even with the looting, arson, and the assaulting of police officers, one of the most shocking scenes was from Charlotte, North Carolina, where BLM supporters chanted "F--- your Jesus!" repeatedly as they marched down the city streets.[1]

Even with our long history of racial division in this country, there have always been believers on both sides. Jesus, it seemed, was the one subject we could all agree on. He's Jesus. He loves us. He died for us. He made a way home for us. And He's coming back soon. We might worship separately. We might think differently about certain points of theology and church order. And we might play different music when we worship Him—but we all worship Him. Right?

While I don't condone the language or the spirit in which that BLM chant was uttered, it does serve as a reminder that although white and black believers in the US claim to worship the same Jesus, far too often there has been "your" Jesus and "our" Jesus. For a long time in popular culture, Jesus was depicted as essentially white. He had white features—light skin tone, blue eyes, sometimes even blonde hair. This version of Jesus is, of course, historically inaccurate, but more than just being sloppy history, this Jesus sent a devastating message to black Christians: "Jesus is ours, not yours."

I bring this up because, more than anything, I want there to be greater unity in the body of Christ. I want Christians of all backgrounds and colors to be able to come together and worship the same Jesus—the Jesus of the Bible.

It's somewhat ironic that the "F--- your Jesus!" chant emanated from Charlotte, North Carolina, as Charlotte is the birthplace of Billy Graham, a man who understood that equality and the gospel go hand in hand.

Preaching in Johannesburg, South Africa, Graham told a crowd of tens of thousands:

Now, Jesus was a man. He was human. He was not a

white man. He was not a black man. He came from that part of the world that touches Africa and Asia and Europe. And He probably had brown skin. Christianity is not a white man's religion. And don't let anybody ever tell you that it's white or black. Christ belongs to all people! He belongs to the whole world![2]

Graham didn't believe there should be one Jesus for the white church and another one for the black church. In fact, he believed there should be no separation between white believers and black believers at all. Before an evangelistic crusade in Chattanooga, Tennessee, in 1953—three years before Martin Luther King Jr. became a national figure and more than a decade before the Civil Rights Act became law —Graham personally went up into the stands and removed the ropes separating the white and black sections of the arena. Given the climate of the country in 1953, what Graham did was somewhat amazing. On the other hand, given the Bible's clear teaching on the unity we should have in Christ and the dignity of all people, it should never have been the exception to the rule.

Today, stadiums aren't segregated according to race, but there's still a lot of work to do. We need more Billy Grahams, more white pastors who are willing to take a stand for unity and equality—to march up the aisles and take down the ropes of separation. Graham was not very popular with many whites in the South on account of his public stand against racism. He was labeled an "integrationist" and a "nigger lover" for what he said and did.[3] But he had learned not to care what people think. He decided instead he must live out the gospel in every way.

Graham wasn't a perfect man. He made mistakes. He fell short. He let people down. But he tried to do the right thing. Today, we need thousands—nay, millions—of Billy Grahams in this country. White men and women who make their voices heard when they see injustice, who take down the ropes, and who work to tear down boundaries. This, of course, doesn't mean buying into the mainstream media narrative about race. For example, the media ignores the correlation between BLM protests and spikes in murder rates[4] or the high percentage of black-on-black crime in inner-cities.[5] At the same time, we are told that the greatest single threat to young black men are the police[6], a statement that is simply untrue.

As believers, we are to be people who champion the truth. That is why we preach the gospel and that is why we stand for justice. We need to remember that we can oppose the BLM movement with its Marxist roots and anarchistic designs while still affirming the dignity of all people. In other words, we can say loudly that black lives matter without affirming Black Lives Matter.

When Paul stood on Mars Hill in Athens and addressed many of the sages and philosophers of the city, he told them:

The God who made the world and everything in it is the Lord of heaven and earth and does not live in temples built by human hands. And he is not served by human hands, as if he needed anything. Rather, he himself gives everyone life and breath and everything else. From one man he made all the nations, that they should inhabit the whole earth; and he marked out their appointed times in history and the boundaries of their lands. God did this so that they would seek him and perhaps reach out for him and find him, though he is not far from any one of us. "For in him we live and move and have our being." As some of your own poets have said, "We are his offspring." (Acts 17:24–28)

The important point for our discussion is that Scripture teaches all people came from Adam. That means that race is superficial. While we may have different genetic traits, different skin colors, and come from different cultures, we are all one race: the race of Adam.

Going back to the Old Testament, we discover that the ancient nations of the world were formed after the Tower of Babel incident. The early people of the world had settled in Shinar (Babylon) in defiance of God's command to "fill the earth and subdue it" (Genesis 1:28). They then built a city and a tower to reach the heavens. Such was an attempt to return to Eden on their own terms—without waiting for the Savior God had promised (see Genesis 3:15).

But the LORD came down to see the city and the tower the people were building. The LORD said, "If as one people speaking the same language they have begun to do this, then nothing they plan to do will be impossible for them. Come, let us go down and confuse their language so they will not understand each other."

So the LORD scattered them from there over all the earth, and they stopped building the city. That is why it was called Babel—because there the LORD confused the language of the whole world. From there the LORD scattered them over the face of the whole earth. (Genesis 11:5–9)

This passage is important in any discussion of race, because it explains how we became fragmented by tribe, tongue, and nation. It shows that our division is not natural or part of the original, good world God created but is instead a consequence of humanity's sin. We should not be surprised, then, to find that when Jesus came, it was to create a new nation made of people from "every nation, tribe, people and language" (Revelation 7:9). As Peter wrote to a group of Christians from many different backgrounds, "But you are a chosen people, a royal priesthood, a holy nation, God's special possession, that you may declare the praises of him who called you out of darkness into his wonderful light" (1 Peter 2:9). *A holy nation.* That's "a," as in singular, one. In Christ, we are all members of one nation, the kingdom of God.

This journey through Scripture is not some arbitrary rabbit trail. I believe that understanding where we've come from and where we're going is essential to maintaining a biblical worldview. This isn't just interesting trivia from the Bible. It's how we are to live today. If white ministers really believed that their black brothers and sisters were just that —their brothers and sisters—our country would be a very different place.

IN THE DIVISIVE world we live in, a lot of pastors, both white and black, are concerned with maintaining unity in their churches. As a result, many refrain from making political statements of any kind from the pulpit. On the one hand, there is great wisdom in this. Our calling is to preach the gospel, to teach the Scriptures, and to equip the flock that has been entrusted to us. It would be a dangerous and foolish thing to connect Jesus to a political candidate, party, or issue.

There are, however, a couple of problems with this line of thinking. First, this is America, a nation of the people, by the people, and for the people. We are self-governing, responsible for choosing our own leaders and lawmakers. That means, in order to be good stewards of the power we have, we must know about the issues. As believers, we can't just do a bit of research and then pick the position that seems best to us. Rather, we must consider every political issue through the lens of Scripture. One of the jobs of a pastor, then, is to help people do their politics as ambassadors of God's kingdom.

Issues surrounding race, justice, and abortion are not morally neutral. As we've already seen, the Bible has a lot to say on those topics. We have to talk about them. Remember, one of the reasons we have Scripture is "so that the servant of God may be thoroughly equipped for every good work" (2 Timothy 3:17). Those good works include speaking up for the innocent unborn and building bridges to the black community.

Pastor Mark Campbell, writing about the reasons some pastors refuse to address the issue of abortion, says this:

> I'm always shocked every time I hear these words uttered, but it happens more than I'd like to admit. A good friend of mine said, "If your church believes this is primarily a political issue, who taught them that? You're the teacher. Correct them."[7]

The second reason we can't afford to be silent on topics like CRT and abortion is that they only become political because they have a moral foundation, and people are divided about the correct moral stance to take. But the Bible speaks clearly on both the sanctity of life and the inherent worth of all people. Regrettably, the pro-life cause is seen as a right-wing issue, while racial justice is seen as a left-wing concern. By taking a stance on either issue, people reflexively take sides. But political platforms do not drive our sermons; the Word of God does. Mark Campbell explains one way to avoid being labeled a political preacher:

> John Piper shared with me in an interview that he experienced the pressure of not wanting to be a partisan, politically-oriented preacher. Yet he saw a beautiful opportunity to address this tension.
>
> Martin Luther King Jr. Day and the anniversary of the Supreme Court's decision in *Roe v. Wade* fall back to back. So Piper decided to preach a sermon every year on racial harmony and the Gospel, and the following week, a sermon on abortion and the Gospel. This way, he preached one weekend on an issue typically associated with the political left, while the next weekend, preaching on an issue that is associated with the right.
>
> He explained that this gave him an opportunity every year to explain to his church that the Word of God is the standard of truth, not a political ideology or camp. As citizens of God's kingdom, we preach the truth, regardless of whether it sounds right- or leftward leaning.[8]

By choosing to be apolitical, pastors are actually letting politics dictate their preaching. They wind up teaching only select parts of God's Word while failing to contextualize the revelation of God so that it might do its work in our generation, and that plays into the enemy's hands.

YEARS AGO, it was common for people to say something to the effect of, "I'm colorblind. I try not to see color. I just treat people as people." The intention might have been to behave as though we live in a society in which people of all races are seen as equals, and thereby usher such a society into being. However, there really is no such thing as colorblindness when it comes to race, nor should we pretend there is. God made the tones of our skin, and He made them beautiful. We can treat other people with dignity and respect without ignoring their skin color.

Like it or not, a person's identity is, in part, wrapped up in their skin color. The way we look is not separate from who we are. It's part of our heritage; it's not incidental. Church planter Cole Brown puts it this way:

When one person tells a person of another ethnicity, "I don't see color," they might as well be saying, "I don't see that part of you that is incredibly important to you and your culture, your family history, your life experience, and your personal identity." This is the equivalent of saying, "I don't see you"—intended or not.[9]

Instead of pretending we're colorblind, it would be better to recognize our diversity but do so without judgment or prejudice. That's what equality looks like. In the book of Revelation, we read:

> After this I looked, and there before me was a great multitude that no one could count, from every nation, tribe, people and language, standing before the throne and before the Lamb. They were wearing white robes and were holding palm branches in their hands. (Revelation 7:9)

In John's vision, he saw a large crowd people before Jesus' throne, and they came from every nation, background, and people group. But here's the kicker: although they formed one new nation, their individual identities hadn't been erased. John could still see their differences. The beauty of the diversity God weaved into the DNA of His human family was still there. Our goal, then, should never be to imagine or try to create a world where everyone is just like us. Instead, we should recognize our differences and celebrate goodness wherever we find it. Latasha Morrison, in her book, *Be the Bridge*, writes: "In the love of the family of God, we must become color brave, color caring, color honoring, and not color blind. We have to recognize the image of God in one another. We have to love despite, and even because of, our differences."[10]

Here's what that can mean practically for all of us, but especially for white ministers:

1. **Work to improve communication:** What you say and what you don't say communicates an awful lot to your congregation. Be clear about what the Bible teaches about race, abortion, and justice. Don't be afraid to stand on the Word of God. And don't be afraid to say "I don't know" when someone asks you a tough question about a complicated issue. Learn together. Grow together.

2. **Seek out relationships with black pastors and black people in your community:** The only way to love someone is to know them, so go out of your way to make friends with *all* brothers and sisters in Christ. Get to know them, listen more than you speak, share your heart, share a meal, and be a friend. Above all, remember Jesus' command: "So in everything, do to others what you would have them do to you" (Matthew 7:12).

3. **Build bridges wherever you can:** There is a lot that divides us, but as followers of Jesus, there is more that unites us. Don't forget that. Even so, when there are differences of opinion and you

can't see eye to eye, do the hard work of building a bridge. Be gracious and curious, and never forget the love of Jesus that has made you both part of the family of God.

4. **Speak up:** It seems like no more than a few days go by before there's another national news story involving race. When it's clear an injustice has been done to someone of another race, don't be silent. Speak up and name it, and if possible, advocate for change. It can mean the world to your black brothers and sisters to know they are seen and that you're on their side.

WHEN JESUS WAS BEATEN and bloody from torture, He was forced to carry His own cross to the place of His execution. But at a certain point, Jesus was no longer able to do it. He was exhausted and without the physical strength to continue. That's when the soldiers seized a stranger from the crowd and forced him to carry the cross (Matthew 27:32). The man they chose was Simon of Cyrene. The city of Cyrene was in North Africa, so most likely, Simon was black.

Scripture doesn't tell us if Simon realized what was happening or who Jesus even was, but there are clues that indicate he likely did at some point. Mark calls him "a certain man from Cyrene, Simon, the father of Alexander and Rufus" (Mark 15:21). The fact that Mark mentions Simon's children tells us that his audience may have known them. Tradition says that Mark wrote his gospel to the Christians in Rome. Interestingly, Romans 16:13 mentions a man named Rufus, who was a member of the church in Rome. While we can't be certain that this Rufus was Simon of Cyrene's son, it wouldn't be too much of stretch to think Simon became a follower of Jesus after that divinely appointed meeting and that he then led his boys to worship Him as well.

Why do I bring all this up? Because I imagine that as Simon was yanked from the crowd and forced to lug that old rugged cross down the dusty streets of Jerusalem, following in the footsteps of a convicted criminal, those who looked on must have pitied him. The poor soul was doing work normally reserved for murderers and insurrectionists. He was, in that moment, the lowest of the low. But in God's eyes, he was taking part in the greatest plot twist the world has ever known. The instrument of death in his hands was the key to unlocking freedom for the human race. Simon was given the privilege of helping the Son of God. He got to bear the cross that took away our sins. He likely got to see the pain in Jesus' eyes as He contemplated the wrath of God that was about to be poured out on Him.

Simon's humble act was in service to the King of kings. This goes to show that things are not always what they seem. In your eyes, someone's appearance may conjure stereotypes and prejudices, perhaps subconsciously, but know this: the greatest servants of King Jesus don't often come wrapped in fine clothes and the prestige of this world. So treat everyone you meet as though they are a member of the King's inner circle. They just might be.

"The reason that we're seeing so many people flee the Left - I like to call them liberal refugees, like myself - is because they do not allow you to think freely. If you agree with them 95 percent and disagree on 5 percent, you are essentially excommunicated. You're not allowed to be a liberal anymore. You're not allowed to be a Democrat anymore."

–Candace Owens

CHAPTER 6
STOCKHOLM SYNDROME

It was a Thursday morning in Sweden's capital city when Jan-Erik Olsson crossed the street and entered Sveriges Kreditbanken. The bank was busy that day, but Olsson decided not to wait in line. He wasn't there to make a deposit or cash a check. Actually, he didn't have an account there at all. Olsson was there for business of a different sort. Pulling a submachine gun from the folded jacket he held in his arms, Olsson raised it above his head and fired several rounds into the ceiling. Then, using his best fake American accent, he shouted to the frightened customers, "The party has just begun!"

Olsson soon made his demands known to the authorities. He wanted $700,000 in cash, a getaway car, and the release of his friend and fellow convict, Clark Olofsson. Within hours, he had everything he wanted, including Olofsson. But there was one stipulation the authorities wouldn't agree to: Olson had wanted to leave the bank with several hostages as insurance that the police wouldn't open fire. The police would not allow the pair to put innocent lives in harm's way during their escape.

And so, a days-long standoff began, with Olsson and Olofsson hunkered down in a bank vault along with several hostages. Before long, captors and captives forged an unmistakable bond. Olsson lent a female hostage his jacket when she got cold. He let another hostage leave the vault when she complained of claustrophobia (though she was still attached by a rope around her waist). Olsson and Olofsson treated their hostages with respect and concern, and in response, the hostages began to identify with their abductors. Soon, everyone was on a first-name basis. It was a strange thing. As the days dragged on, the hostages were more concerned that the police might harm them than they were that Olsson or Olofsson might.

On the sixth day, police pumped tear gas into the vault, and the two criminals finally surrendered. But even then, the hostages insisted on staying behind to ensure the safety of Olsson and Olofsson. At the vault door, hostage takers and hostages embraced as they said goodbye to one another. One hostage, as she was being wheeled away on a stretcher, cried out to Olofsson, "Clark, I will see you again!" The scene seemed so bizarre to onlookers. No one could quite understand what had happened. For that matter, the hostages themselves didn't quite understand it. One even went to a psychiatrist the following day because she couldn't figure out why she didn't hate the two men who had held her captive. She just knew she didn't.

In the days that followed, this strange phenomena became known as Stockholm Syndrome, a term that still used today whenever a victim develops an affection for their oppressor.[1] I share this origin story, because I've seen Stockholm Syndrome cast its spell over large segments of the black community. I've watched as otherwise reasonable and self-respecting men and women have lined up to cast their votes for a political party that takes them for granted. I've listened as friends have echoed the Marxist talking points of the Black Lives Matter movement. And I've mourned the millions of children who have been tossed away because their community believes abortion is a socially responsible option. For too long, black Christian leaders have made excuses for our oppressors, championing the very policies and philosophies that keep our people in chains. It seems Stockholm Syndrome is alive and well.

Since 1968, not a single Republican candidate for president of the United States has received more than a 13-percent share of the black vote. More than 80 percent of black voters in the US self-identify as Democrats. And yet, blacks comprise the most conservative voting bloc within the Democratic Party.

This partisan loyalty is maintained through a strategic social process that we call racialized social constraint, whereby support for the Democratic Party has come to be defined as a norm of group behavior. In other words, supporting the Democratic Party has come to be understood as just something you do as a black person, an expectation of behavior meant to empower the racial group.

Adherence with this norm of Democratic Party support is insured through a set of social rewards and penalties which recognize compliance and punish defection of racial group members. Interestingly, it is the social and spatial segregation of black Americans that makes all this work. It is through racially segregated spaces that blacks become aware of the importance of the party norm for the racial group. And it is within these segregated spaces that social rewards for compliance and penalties for defection can come to define an individual's social status within the group. The result of all this is that to the extent that any individual black American values their relationship with other black Americans, they will continue to act in accordance with the group norm of party support lest they find themselves socially isolated.[2]

I've seen this strange but powerful phenomena up close plenty of times, but no matter how many times I see it, I'm still shocked by it. A few years ago, I was waiting for a haircut at the barber shop when I struck up a conversation with another customer. It started out as small talk, but before long our discussion turned to issues of substance. Soon, I had mentioned my views on abortion and how I believed that life begins in the womb. After I explained I was pro-life, this gentleman—a black man—looked at me with disdain in his eyes. It was as though I had insulted him personally. I knew in that moment our friendly conversation was over. He told me the pro-life cause was "a white man's issue" and said I shouldn't waste my time.

Though I fight for unborn children of all races, I am especially mindful of the damage being done to black communities. Abortion is certainly not a white man's issue. But because this stranger in the barber shop was trapped in a form of Stockholm Syndrome, he considered me a traitor to our community.

In 1852, Frederick Douglass delivered a speech entitled "What, to a Slave, Is the Fourth of July?" Douglass, who had grown up a slave and suffered cruelly at the whip of white taskmasters, knew that the promise of this country had not yet been realized in his day:

> What, to the American slave, is your Fourth of July? I answer: a day that reveals to him, more than all other days in the year, the gross injustice and cruelty to which he is the constant victim. To him, your celebration is a

sham; your boasted liberty, an unholy license; your national greatness, swelling vanity; your sounds of rejoicing are empty and heartless; your denunciations of tyrants, brass fronted impudence; your shouts of liberty and equality, hollow mockery; your prayers and hymns, your sermons and thanksgivings, with all your religious parade, and solemnity, are, to him, mere bombast, fraud, deception, impiety, and hypocrisy—a thin veil to cover up crimes which would disgrace a nation of savages. There is not a nation on the earth guilty of practices, more shocking and bloody, than are the people of these United States, at this very hour.[3]

Though Douglass had grown up in a world where he was considered another man's property, he eventually escaped slavery and became a prominent abolitionist. But the change in his physical situation only came about because of a change in his mental and spiritual condition. When Douglass was a young boy, one of his masters' wives taught him the alphabet. With the letters of the English language at his disposal, he taught himself how to read and write. Soon, he was teaching other slaves to read, using the Bible as his textbook. Literacy and Scripture helped Douglass to see himself as more than a slave, to break through the spell his white masters had placed him under. He knew he was more than property, more than an unpaid servant or a beast of burden—he was a child of God.

But there was something else Douglass knew. He knew that, at its core, the United States of America was a good place, or at least it could be. The seeds of freedom and opportunity for all people—white, black, and every other color—were sown into the founding documents like seeds that would one day sprout when the time was right:

> Fellow Citizens, I am not wanting in respect for the fathers of this republic. The signers of the Declaration of Independence were brave men. They were great men too —great enough to give fame to a great age....
>
> With them, nothing was "settled" that was not right. With them, justice, liberty and humanity were "final;" not slavery and oppression. You may well cherish the memory of such men. They were great in their day and generation. Their solid manhood stands out the more as we contrast it with these degenerate times....
>
> Now, take the Constitution according to its plain reading, and I defy the presentation of a single pro-slavery clause in it. On the other hand it will be found to contain principles and purposes, entirely hostile to the existence of slavery.[4]

Though Frederick Douglass was a powerful leader who did much to promote the cause of freedom for black Americans, his rhetoric would be out of step with most of today's black leaders. Instead of seeing hope in America's history, they see shame. Instead of seeing promise in America's future, they see an unending cycle of white supremacy and systemic racism. But if anyone could speak of "systemic racism," it was Douglass. If anyone could complain about a lack of equality (or "equity"), it was Douglass. If anyone could suppose that the history books needed to be rewritten, it was Douglass. And yet, he believed that America still held promise for the future—that the nation's best days were ahead.

Douglass found optimism in the Founding Fathers. He knew that they weren't joking when the they wrote that "all men are created equal." He knew that "life, liberty, and the pursuit of happiness" truly were "unalienable rights," even if he did not know them personally. So, rather than focusing on the dismal reality the land of the free had become in his day, he worked to change the nation so that it might, one day, live up to the promises made by its founders.

But Douglass also looked to the Scriptures. He understood the deeper truth: that no law upholding slavery and no whip from a cruel taskmaster could make him a slave. He was free, because Christ had set him free:

Douglass took few possessions on his long journey to freedom. He left behind his chains, but not his prophetic Christian faith that first took root in slavery. At the foundation of that faith rested certain assurances: that God suffers with the oppressed and will not tolerate injustice forever; that slaveholders perverted the Christian faith in their religious justifications of oppression; that Christ, in bidding all to come and die, offers a new way to live, radically different from the world's hatred and violence.[5]

Although Douglass escaped slavery on his own terms and even lived to see the Emancipation Proclamation signed by President Lincoln, he did not have to wait until the federal government of the United States ended slavery in order to be free. He refused to accept the narrative his captors preached: that black people were an inferior race, that he and his brothers and sisters were created by God to serve whites, and that things would always be the way they were. In other words, he refused to be trapped by Stockholm Syndrome.

While slavery is far in the rearview mirror, many blacks today have a terrible case of Stockholm Syndrome. Their captors may not carry whips, but they are kept in chains just the same. It is the programs and policies of the Democratic Party that are largely responsible for the breakdown of the family, the cyclical poverty many blacks experience, and the hatred of white people so prevalent in black communities. And yet, most blacks are loyal Democrats, returning election after election to vote for Democratic candidates and the failed platforms they represent.

For example, socialized education, propped up by the

Democrat-led teachers' unions, delivers Leftist classrooms and inferior schools to black neighborhoods, while school choice—a concept championed by many Republicans—would give black parents the opportunity to send their children to the schools of their choosing, be they the best public schools in the area, local Christian schools, or college-preparatory private schools. But rather than fighting for the freedom of choice, most blacks go along with the policies of their captors.

THINK BACK to the original Stockholm Syndrome story for a moment. Consider the hostages in that bank vault in Stockholm. They somehow found an affection for the convicts who were keeping them there against their will, under threat of certain death. As difficult as that is to imagine, their calm and supportive demeanor went a long way to keeping them safe. The alternative—openly hostile rebellion—might have cost them their lives.

Stockholm Syndrome, then, has this appeal: it's often the safe road. That's why many slaves in the United States were compliant and even affectionate toward their masters. If slavery is all a person has ever known, and there is no foreseeable path to escape, that person's survival instinct kicks in. They begin to cope in whatever way they can. I believe that may be what's happened to many people in the black community today. It doesn't seem like there's a way out of their plight, so they have learned to cope by acquiescing to their oppressors. But I want to suggest there is another way—a third option that doesn't require giving in to the seduction of Stockholm Syndrome or falling prey to the tyranny of an angry heart.

In ancient Rome, slavery wasn't race-based as it was in the United States. Typically, people became slaves through debt. The slaves of the wealthy actually exercised a good deal of authority, regularly getting the opportunity to act on their master's behalf. As a result, many were comfortable, often faring better than free men. Of course, that wasn't always the case. Slavery could be harsh, and it always meant the loss of personal freedom.

Onesimus was a slave, and his master was quite wealthy. But Onesimus still wanted to be free. In fact, he wanted his freedom so badly that he risked his life running away from his master, Philemon. That's because, according to Roman law, a runaway slave could be killed by his master; it was a serious crime. But Onesimus wanted out. So he left Colossae and headed to the city of Rome. It was there, in the capital city of the empire, that Onesimus met a man named Paul. The apostle Paul was a prisoner, and yet somehow, miraculously, he crossed paths with Onesimus. It's likely the two had met before, since Paul knew Philemon. But it was in Rome that Paul introduced Onesimus, the runaway slave, to Jesus Christ.

Here's the remarkable thing: now that Onesimus was a believer, Paul didn't tell him about the evils of slavery and send him on his way to continue his journey of freedom. Instead, he instructed Onesimus to return home to Philemon. But he sent him with a letter for his master. In it, Paul asked Philemon to welcome Onesimus "no longer as a slave, but better than a slave, as a dear brother" (Philemon 16). He could say that because Onesimus had become a follower of Christ. He had transferred his citizenship from this world, where he was not a true citizen but a slave, to the kingdom of God, where he was not just a citizen but a son of the King.

Along with the personal letter to Philemon, Paul tucked away another letter in the pack of his new spiritual son, Onesimus—the letter we know today as Colossians. In that letter, Paul wrote the following:

> Slaves, obey your earthly masters in everything; and do it, not only when their eye is on you and to curry their favor, but with sincerity of heart and reverence for the Lord. Whatever you do, work at it with all your heart, as working for the Lord, not for human masters, since you know that you will receive an inheritance from the Lord as a reward. It is the Lord Christ you are serving. Anyone who does wrong will be repaid for their wrongs, and there is no favoritism.
>
> Masters, provide your slaves with what is right and

fair, because you know that you also have a Master in heaven. (Colossians 3:22–4:1)

This passage is jarring for modern readers who know that slavery is an abomination. No person should be considered property. All people are made in the image of God and should be treated with the dignity that such a status provides. And yet, Paul instructed slaves to obey their masters. Why? Because he knew that the gospel brought with it the seeds to one day destroy slavery. It was an institution that would crumble under the weight of the kingdom of God, all on its own. A person cannot follow Jesus' command to love their neighbor while keeping their neighbor in bondage. It simply won't work. So Paul can write confidently that, in the meantime, slaves should do their work as though they are working for Jesus, and masters should treat their slaves the way they would if Jesus were watching—because He is.

I bring this up because it represents a way to break free from Stockholm Syndrome while yielding fully to the Lord, rather than a new master of anger, rage, and hatred. Onesimus did not return to his master as a victim, nor did he regard Philemon as his enemy. Despite the injustice of slavery and everything else that was in their past, Onesimus determined to embrace Philemon as a brother. He wasn't putting blinders on to go back to the way things were, nor was he going to return evil for evil. He walked home with love and forgiveness in his heart, holding out a new way forward for himself and for his master. If we keep our eyes on Jesus and place our hope in His kingdom, we can be free, despite our circumstances.

At the same time, we are not called to be complacent. In another letter, Paul wrote, "Were you a slave when you were called? Don't let it trouble you—although if you can gain your freedom, do so" (1 Corinthians 7:21). Because of the Constitution and the Bill of Rights, we have the opportunity to gain our freedom from the tyranny of Leftist propaganda and policies. We do not have to remain in slavery. We are a self-governing people who can make real change by using our voices and our votes.

Today, many black Americans champion the Marxist ideas found in critical race theory, because they believe it is a way forward. But we don't have to take on the yoke of Marxism in an attempt to make a better world for ourselves and our children and grandchildren. (Marxism *never* brings about a better world anyway.) Likewise, we don't have to let the abortion industry bring an ongoing genocide to our communities. We can choose life and do the hard work of raising godly children who serve the Lord and further the kingdom of God.

For far too long, the Democratic Party has taken the black community for granted. Democratic politicians don't actually serve the black constituents they represent, because they have reasonable and demonstrable certainty that, no matter how they govern or what policies they put forward, blacks will continue to vote their way. In effect, by voting so consistently, black Americans have silenced their own political voice.

MANNING JOHNSON WAS A BLACK MAN, and he was also a member of the Communist party. For ten long years, he was a Communist, serving in a variety of roles. He was the district agitation propaganda director in Buffalo, New York from 1931–1932. Then he ran as the Communist Party candidate for the United States House of Representatives in New York's twenty-second congressional district. So, when he left the Communist Party in 1939 and devoted the rest of his life to helping blacks break through the fog of Stockholm Syndrome, he knew what he was talking about.

He exposed much of what he saw in order to expose the grift being foisted on black Americans:

> A large number of Negro ministers are all for the Communists. Some are prominent and influential; others are "run of the mill." They in common believe that beating the racial drums is a short cut to prominence, money and the realization of personal ambitions even if the Negro masses are left prostrate and bleeding— expendables in the mad scramble for power. . . .

The bulk of Negro church members are in the South. They live by the "Good Book." Anyone against the "Good Book" is of the devil. There is no in between. The Red carpet-baggers discovered this when they touched the Negro's religion. So they avoided this sore spot in order to snare their intended victims. Get them involved in the movement first and later do the job on their religious convictions was the order. Anything else was putting the cart before the horse.

The new line went like this: Jesus, the carpenter, was a worker like the Communists. He was against the "money changers," the "capitalists," the "exploiters" of that day. That is why he drove them from the temple. The Communists are the modern day fighters against the capitalists or money changers. If Jesus were living today, he would be persecuted like the Communists who seek to do good for the common people.[6]

Today, it's not the Communist Party but the Democratic Party, though the tactics and the desired outcomes are largely the same. Leftists seek to use black people for their own purposes. They are not interested in improving the lives of people of color. Their policies and programs might create a certain "floor" of economic stability, but there is little for black Americans to hold onto that would assist them in climbing the social and economic ladder. In that way, the current situation bears a striking resemblance to plantation life under slavery.

Inner-cities are the domain of Democratic politicians. Just look at an electoral map, and you'll see that most of the large cities in America are bright blue, even in otherwise red states. And it is in these inner-cities that most blacks find themselves trapped, not unlike their ancestors on the plantations of the old South. Conservative author and film-maker Dinesh D'Souza explains the parallels:

I was actually reading a book by the historian Kenneth Stampp, and it's on the old slave plantation. It's called *The Peculiar Institution*. And he describes the five features of the slave plantation. I think this is really interesting because all the five features he mentions are present today, but they're present on the urban plantations that the democrats are running in the inner cities. And so Kenneth Stampp says number one on the typical old slave plantation you have ramshackle dwellings. Houses but they're in disarray. Second you have the family structure is all broken down, a lot if illegitimacy, whose kids are whose, you don't really know, that's the nature of slavery. Third, a lot of the violence that's necessary to hold the— to keep the place together—because slavery is based on coercion, you have to force people, you have to whip them, beat them, etc. Fourth, everybody has a minimum provision. You get food, you get health care, but nobody gets ahead. Nobody gets a good education. No ladders of opportunity. Nihilism, hopelessness, and despair.

So you take all these elements and ask, "How's it really different today in inner city Oakland, or Detroit, or Chicago?" I think the main difference is that in the old days the Democrats who ran those slave plantations too, wanted to steal people's labor. They wanted labor, and they wanted labor for free. Now what they want is votes. They want votes, and they don't care about these people. And that's why they remain in misery and the Democrats are perfectly happy to keep them there as long as they keep voting, eighty to ninety percent, for the party that's running the plantation.[7]

Every American ought to be skeptical of politicians' promises. Our system is one in which their jobs are contingent upon our votes. It's a wonderful system insofar as it provides an incentive for government officials to keep their promises, govern fairly, and serve the nation well. However, one need only look at our country's inner-cities to see that the Left has either been lying or is completely incompetent. Although I believe the lies are intentional and blatant, for a moment let's give the Democrats the benefit of the doubt and assume their motives are good. The lack of solid results tell us they're not up to the job. They cannot be trusted to run our cities, our counties, our states, or our nation.

Critical race theory is but one more tool to keep the plantation going. It promises a solution to the problem of racism, but it doesn't actually address the root causes of cyclical poverty or prejudice. Proponents of CRT attack white people en masse for the crime of being white while ignoring—and in many cases, exacerbating—the very real problems facing black Americans.

IT'S INTERESTING that Manning Johnson pointed out the use of Scripture in Communist propaganda. The Communists wanted blacks to read the Gospels through a modern political grid, transposing workers for Jesus and capitalists for moneychangers. In their version, Jesus is on the side of the working class, a Communist activist, and the capitalists are His enemies. But in truth, Jesus' politics transcended our earthly political parties. The kingdom is always higher, always more real, and always our true hope.

Like Onesimus before us, we don't have to fall under the trance of Stockholm Syndrome, romanticizing and colluding with our captors, nor do we have to give in to rage and bitterness, as though evil can be extinguished with more evil. We can, instead, work for change on earth while our hearts are firmly fixed on heaven. How? By seeking out truth—not falling for easy answers, political arguments, or vicious lies designed to appeal to our sinful hearts.

One of the privileges of freedom, according to our nation's Founding Fathers, is the ability to seek out truth. That's what all that stuff about freedom of speech, freedom of expression, and freedom of religion was all about. They understood that truth, handled well, is a powerful weapon. It shatters lies, dispels darkness, and invites enduring love. We would do well to remember, there is no Stockholm Syndrome in true love. "Love does not delight in evil but rejoices with the truth" (1 Corinthians 13:6).

"Those on the left who scream about income gaps choose to focus on the success of those at the top rather than the failures of those at the bottom. They conveniently ignore that liberals are the ones who have pushed the moral relativism and welfare-state dependence that has destroyed black families over the last 60 years. And it is these same liberals who fight to keep low-income kids in failing public schools and fight efforts to get school choice."

–Star Parker

CHAPTER 7
WHAT ABOUT THE CHILDREN?

In the beginning, there was a garden. That garden was the place where heaven and earth met. And so, as you might expect, peace filled the air, but so did beauty and truth, joy and praise. There was harmony between the first humans, the creation, and God Himself. It was very good—all of it.

The Bible doesn't tell us how long Edenic bliss lasted. But no matter how long it was, it wasn't nearly long enough. The serpent enticed Eve to sin, and the woman invited her husband, Adam, to join her. The pair disobeyed the Lord, and sin entered our world, bringing every imaginable evil with it. Every heartache and loss has its root in that crunch of forbidden fruit. Death now stalks us, demanding to quench its insatiable appetite. The world's goodness, while not destroyed, came unraveled.

But God's judgment also came with a promise. As He was condemning the serpent, He said, "And I will put enmity between you and the woman, and between your offspring and hers; he will crush your head, and you will strike his heel" (Genesis 3:15). A Child would come, a Son who would destroy the evil one. This Child would be a Deliverer, a Savior, and He would undo the curse wrought in Eden.

I'm sure Adam's and Eve's ears perked up at this striking prophecy from the mouth of the Lord. *There is hope!* they must have thought to themselves. *It's not too late to repair the damage we've done!* But the announcement must have grabbed the serpent's attention as well. His demise would come from the crushing blow of a Child. Ever since, the serpent—whom the Bible later reveals to be Satan (see Revelation 12:9)—has had it in for the children of humanity.

It's not a coincidence that Pharaoh ordered the murder of newborn Hebrew boys as God's people cried out for a deliverer. It's not by happenstance that Herod ordered the slaughter of all the male children under the age of two living in the vicinity of Bethlehem after he learned from the wise men that a new star had appeared in the sky to announce the birth of a newborn King. It's not by chance that child sacrifice became a prominent feature of many ancient pagan rituals. And it's not a fluke of history that abortion has killed more than 64 million babies since the

Roe v. Wade Supreme Court decision of 1973.[1] As Jesus Himself said, the devil "was a murderer from the beginning" (John 8:44). Even though he knows he has been defeated and his final judgment is near, he hasn't changed a bit.

IN BUFFALO, New York, fifth graders are being taught lessons from the Black Lives Matter playbook, including the need to disrupt the traditional, nuclear family as the primary unit of society.[2] In Oregon, K–12 teachers are being trained to confront "the toxic characteristics of white supremacy culture with respect to math."[3] In Cupertino, California, third-graders were asked to "deconstruct their racial identities, then rank themselves according to their 'power and privilege.'"[4] Hundreds of elementary classrooms across the country include in their curriculum the book *Not My Idea: A Book about Whiteness,* which depicts a white person dressed as a devil and teaches students that they need to sign away their whiteness.[5] The list could go on and on, but the picture is clear: critical race theory is coming for our kids.

As we've already seen, CRT teaches black students that the majority, if not all, of their problems, disappointments, and challenges are a result of systemic racism. The message is clear: blacks are the victims, and nothing can change that.

At the same time, white students learn their whiteness is itself a great evil. Everything they enjoy in life was stolen from blacks, indigenous peoples, and other minorities. They learn to hate themselves. Both groups are defined by the color of their skin; it is the most important thing about them.

The goal of CRT is not to heal racial divides that exist in our country, but rather to aggravate them. As commentators Jonathan Butcher and Mike Gonzalez put it:

> [CRT] will not create a national identity that the future lawyers, doctors, and lawmakers—not to mention parents, neighbors, and co-workers—can share. State officials, local school board members, and educators have the power—and the right—to prevent this new material from telling students that there is no America, only tribes competing for power.[6]

Though the message of critical race theory may be internalized by white students and students of color differently, it does tremendous damage to all children.

At its heart, CRT is an accusation. The theory claims white people are inherently and hopelessly racist. Accusation is the realm of Satan. In fact, the Hebrew word behind the devil's name means "accuser." Accusation is his business. It's how he operates in this world. Just think back to the garden. The serpent came to Eve with a temptation that was wrapped in an accusation against the Lord: "God knows that when you eat from it [the fruit of the tree of the knowledge of good and evil] your eyes will be opened, and you will be like God, knowing good and evil" (Genesis 3:5). In other words, "God is holding out on you." Satan's temptation was not so much about the fruit itself, though Eve saw it "was good for food and pleasing to the eye" (v. 6), but about doubting God's goodness.

Though the incident in the garden comes at the beginning of Satan's career as "the accuser of our brothers and sisters" (Revelation 12:10), his tactics never really change. Today, he's using CRT to pit races against one another, and he's not waiting until our children are old enough to think analytically about what they're being taught.

Normally, the best way to silence an accusation is to bring it into the light. If it's false, the truth will destroy it, and if it's a legitimate accusation, confession and repentance will clear a new path forward. But as many parents have discovered, CRT dictates that anyone who questions the truth of systemic racism permeating all of society is, in fact, racist. In other words, if you say you have questions or that you don't believe all American institutions create obstacles for people of color, it's because your own racism has blinded you. Proponents of CRT do not want to discuss the validity of their doctrine; they simply want to silence their detractors. The best way to do that is to label anyone who does not agree with CRT a racist. In that sense, CRT is a new kind of unbending, unflinching fundamentalism that, to its advocates, must be preserved at all costs.

BEFORE PROGRESSIVES BEGAN TINKERING with America's education system in the late nineteenth century, the foundation of our schools was built on something called the Western Christian Paideia. What is *paideia*?

The Greek word for an ancient concept, *Paideia* has no exact English translation. It is essentially the part of upbringing and education that forms the soul of a human being — and it is key to the formation of a culture.[7]

The ancient Greeks discovered that by giving children a certain set of tools and teaching them *how* to think, not *what* to think, they would grow up to be free, whole people who could participate in society. In school, children didn't just learn a trade; they learned how to be fully human. This idea was revolutionary and formed the basis for Western civilization.

With the coming of Christ, the gospel became central to this paideia and changed the lives of millions of people across Europe and on into the New World. It became the Western Christian paideia and focused on the seven liberal[8] arts: grammar, logic, rhetoric, arithmetic, astronomy, music, and geometry. One of the central features of this classical approach to education was its emphasis on history. It was important for students to know where they came from, to learn from the mistakes of the past, and to honor those who made great advances.

Today, when progressives talk about history, what they're really talking about is a certain skewed narrative of history. Take, for example, Howard Zinn's *A People's History of the United States*, arguably the bestselling textbook of all time. In the book, Zinn argues that America was built on land stolen from Native Americans using forced labor stolen from African slaves. He says Columbus was a genocidal maniac, the Founding Fathers fought the American Revolution not for liberty but for their own power and wealth, and the US was no better than Germany in World War II. With such a warped view of history being taught, it's no wonder today's progressives truly hate America!

Zinn is not without his critics. Actual historians have a lot of problems with his take on American history. Dr. Mary Grabar writes:

Zinn did everything—misrepresented sources, omitted critical information, falsified evidence, and plagiarized. . . . Zinn liked to pretend [that] he wrote a 'people's' history, telling the bottom-up story of neglected and forgotten men and women. The problem is that he falsified American history to promote Communist revolution. . . . all the while denying that he was a Communist.[9]

Even so, *A People's History of the United States* continues to be popular and remains gospel to progressives. It does so because its contents fit the narrative they want us all to believe.

No one is arguing that America's history is without sin, but when we teach our children an exaggerated, dishonest version of only the bad stuff, it will have an effect. We've already looked at *The 1619 Project*, a curriculum that teaches America was truly founded, not in 1776 with the Declaration of Independence, but in 1619, when the first African slaves arrived in the Jamestown colony. The goal of the project is not to teach American history fairly and honestly—or even to uncover some darker moments that have been forgotten. Instead, its purpose is to shape the future, one where boys and girls of color will learn to see themselves solely through the tinted lens of victimhood. It's hard to imagine anything more destructive to innocent souls or to our future as a united country than that.

The alternative to a twisted narrative of history is an honest one. All history must be selective, but there is a difference between leaving out less important details in order to provide the essential truths and crafting a version of events that no longer resembles anything like the truth. A Christian view of history—or science or literature or any subject—begins with Jesus Christ, "in whom are hidden all the treasures of wisdom and knowledge" (Colossians 2:3). We must consider history in light of the gospel.

We are all fallen, sinful people, and so, we shouldn't be surprised to find our history contains works of evil. But because of the cross, the story of humanity now has hope. Our past does not define us. We can be made holy. We will not be sinless this side of glory, but we can do better in this generation than we did in the previous one. However, the standard we must always measure by is the unchanging truth of God's Word, not the changing whims of culture.

As we teach our children history, we must decide which history we will teach: a selective narrative masquerading as history that is designed to suit the current political biases of the Left—chock full of half-truths, exaggerations, and full-blooded lies—or history that embraces where we came from and celebrates our heritage without sugarcoating the sins of our ancestors.

After the riots of 2020, it became fashionable to tear down or vandalize statues of historical figures. All across the country, confederate soldiers, slaveholding Founding Fathers, and Christopher Columbus were toppled or marred. While none of this destruction does anything to change what actually happened in history, those who believe we should remove these memorials are, in a sense, erasing history from public view. This is precisely what happens in the classroom when we allow a filtered history bent on getting kids to hate America. The answer, of course, is not to ignore America's sins; it's to learn from them.

When it comes to the statues of less-than-noble figures, Allen Guelzo, a historian from Gettysburg College, reminds us:

> There are injustices that have been swept behind curtains, and which have to be memorialized if we want to talk about a realistic history. The suffering, loss, robbery, the indignity of neglect, these are all parts of our history as well.
>
> In remembering those parts of it, we're adding a dimension of humanity to how we understand ourselves. History is not simply a matter of discovering who was virtuous and who was perfect. It's also a matter of discovering that, humanely speaking, we are full of people who made mistakes. We are full, in our history, of people who took wrong turns.
>
> We're full of moments when unspeakable things were done. We have to remember those, because it's only by remembering them that we actually gain the impetus to do the things that really are virtuous and right and noble. Sometimes we need what has happened in terms of evil to be there to remind us about how absolutely important it is to do the good, and how little we can expect the good to happen automatically.[10]

There's wisdom here that can apply to the classroom as well. We cannot topple the history we don't like and pretend it doesn't exist. We need our history. We need our children to know all the chapters that have come before so they will know where they fit in the story. As Edmund Burke once said, "Those who don't know history are destined to repeat it." No matter our current political persuasion, we should all be able to agree that an honest approach to American history is in the best interest of our kids—and the future of the United States.

ABORTION IS a different sort of attack on our kids. Rather than trying to convert our children into soldiers for a Leftist, "woke" agenda, abortion simply seeks to kill them in the womb. As with all attempted genocides, the impetus is fear. As we saw with Margaret Sanger's twisted ideology, her fear was that black people would ruin the utopia she wanted to construct. There was simply no place in her imagination for a future where white, black, and brown people all live and work together side by side in harmony.

Children who are not aborted do not get to escape the evil of the industry. Progressives make sure of that. Kids today are indoctrinated by an onslaught of propaganda from Hollywood and our educational system to believe that sex outside of marriage is the norm, pregnancy is an inconvenience rather than a serious and solemn responsibility, and abortion is a God-given right, which should always remain convenient and affordable. In essence, the powers that be set our children up to make big mistakes, the scars of which can last a lifetime.

All this is, of course, in sharp contradiction to the teachings of Scripture. When God brought Eve to Adam to be his bride, we read, "That is why a man leaves his father and mother and is united to his wife, and they become one flesh" (Genesis 2:24). Jesus affirmed this design. Sex is to be enjoyed within the bounds of hetero-sexual marriage. Children are a blessing from the Lord within that union. But when children are taught that such restrictions are superficial and run counter to nature, they are given license to sin. Abortion is held up as a pinnacle virtue by many on the Left because they understand it is key to avoiding the consequence of having children outside of marriage. That is why free love doctrine and abortion culture always go hand-in-hand.

If you stop and think about it, the lie of a no-boundaries sexual ethic is really no different from the original lie the serpent whispered to Eve. The premise is exactly the same: the accusation that God is holding out on us. He designed sex to be a wonderful, beautiful, fruitful experience within a loving and stable marriage between a man and a woman. To that, the devil says, "God has lied to you! You're missing out if you aren't having sex whenever, wherever, and with whomever you want."

These days, it's easy to lose count of all the various sexual permutations our culture champions. Between sexual preferences and sexual identities, the possibilities are seemingly unlimited. LGB (Lesbian, Gay, and Bisexual) became LGBT (adding Transgender), and then it grew to LGBTQ (adding Queer), and then LGBTQ+ (to include an unlimited number of identities), and at the time of writing, it's even sprouted to LGBTQIA2S+ (adding Intersex, Asexual, and Two Spirit). Who knows how long the acronym will be by the time this book is published!

The sad reality is this: the progressive machine isn't waiting until children are old enough to think for themselves before unloading this cafeteria of sexual confusion on them. They're coming after our kids when they're young —and they're succeeding. A recent Barna poll revealed that 39 percent of Gen Z now identifies as LGBTQ. Even more shocking: 27 percent of Millennial Christians and 28 percent of born-again Millennial Christians identify as LGBTQ![11]

Is there any wonder progressives parade Drag Queen Story Hour out in front proudly? If you don't know what Drag Queen Story Hour is, it's exactly what it sounds like: a man dressed up as an over-the-top flamboyant female diva, reading stories like *The Hips on the Drag Queen Go Swish, Swish, Swish* to children ages three to eight.[12] Many on the Left argue that a drag queen reading stories to children is harmless fun and serves to break down prejudices while kids are still young, but in reality the events are designed to normalize sexual deviance and raise society's tolerance for perversion. There is nothing harmless about them:

> Drag Queen Story Hour has come under fire in recent years for a number of scandals. In 2018, a Louisiana drag queen who participated in the events admitted to grooming children as young as three. In 2019, photos surfaced of children lying on top of drag queens during the story hour in Portland. That same year, another drag queen was caught exposing himself to children during the event in Minnesota.[13]

At a public school in Enfield, Connecticut, children were given an assignment called "Pizza & Consent," in which they were asked to choose their sexual likes and dislikes as though they were toppings on a pizza:

> The assignment instructed the eighth [sic] graders to explore their sex preferences by drawing and coloring their favorite type of pizza and "mirror these preferences in relation to sex!"
>
> Examples provided included "Likes: Cheese = Kissing" and "Dislikes: Olives = Giving oral."
>
> Below the pizza drawing there appeared space to equate pizza likes and dislikes to sexual acts.[14]

When parents discovered the disgusting and morally bankrupt assignment, they quickly complained. The teacher responsible for posting the assignment said it was an innocent mistake:

> "I caught the error after our curriculum revision in June, but failed to post the intended version," [Brie] Quartin [the district's health and physical education coordinator] said. "I own that, and apologize for the error. The correct version of the assignment is for students to work in small groups to craft a pizza with toppings (no behaviors associated with said toppings) that would make everyone happy/comfortable using non-verbal communication only."[15]

Concerned parents were, of course, skeptical. One parent was quoted as saying, "I'm not sure how a teacher accidentally asks for the personal sexual preferences of 8th-graders without any indication it is completely inappropriate to do such a thing?"[16] But it is not uncommon for progressives to backpedal after doing something so obviously reprehensible. Even when caught red-handed, they will often simply chalk the inappropriate behavior to a mistake and move on.

These are not isolated incidents. It seems everywhere we look these days—from television cartoons to the classroom to their favorite Disney movies, the liberal agenda is pushing to sexualize our kids at younger and younger ages. Why? Because they are hardcore fundamentalists who want to remake the world according to their own values, and chief among their spiritual disciplines are sexual perversion and abortion on demand.

In the black community, this diabolical ethic has contributed to the epidemic of children being born out of wedlock and the near-ubiquitous single-parent homes these children grow up in. The damage has been catastrophic, reinforcing generational poverty and a perpetual cycle of sinful behavior. To make matters worse, if a white person gives their voice to expose this reality, they are soon met with choruses of "Racist!" And if a black person speaks up, they are told they are a sellout, an Uncle Tom, or worse—that they're no longer truly black.

FOR MANY YEARS, the nationwide toy store chain Toys R Us donated a portion of its profits to Planned Parenthood. In 2018, Toys R Us declared bankruptcy and announced the closure of its 735 stores across the United States. It seems a strange thing that a business that thrives by selling toys to small children would make charitable contributions to an organization bent on destroying those same children. It certainly makes you wonder if Toys R Us sowed the seeds of its own business failure by supporting abortion on demand so handily.

I bring up the cautionary tale of Toys R Us because I believe we might be headed down the same path. When it comes to our children, we want to protect them from harm, and yet many of us send them to public schools where we know they will be indoctrinated with a woke ideology, exposed to all manner of sexual perversion, and taught to hate America. Without realizing it, we are sowing the seeds of our children's moral and spiritual failures.

There was once a time when the prayer and the study of the Bible were central to an American education. But that was a long time ago. Prayer is gone. The Bible is gone. God Himself has been told to leave the building. It's no wonder our society has become so godless. As my father-in-law, Bishop Patrick Lane Wooden Sr., likes to say, "If you bar God from a place, that place is cursed." I believe our schools and much of the media aimed at our children are cursed. They're not profitable for our kids and only serve to undermine the faith that we have been charged with passing on to them.

Make no mistake: Satan wants to destroy our children, either in the womb through the brutal practice of abortion or more slowly through our nation's schools and media, which have been overrun by progressives. He hates the image of God and lashes out at humanity because we were made to bear that image. As followers of Jesus, we're in a battle with the evil one, and our children are caught in the middle.

At the close of his letter to the church in Rome, Paul wrote this word of encouragement to the believers there: "The God of peace will soon crush Satan under your feet" (Romans 16:20). This, of course, is an echo of Genesis 3:15. We get to share in Jesus' victory—and so will our children, but we must raise them in the fear and admonition of the Lord. If we do that, Satan's plan for America doesn't stand a chance.

"True prayer is done in secret, but this does not rule out the fellowship of prayer altogether, however clearly we may be aware of its dangers. In the last resort it is immaterial whether we pray in the open street or in the secrecy of our chambers, whether briefly or lengthily, in the Litany of the Church, or with the sigh of one who knows not what he should pray for. True prayer does not depend either on the individual or the whole body of the faithful, but solely upon the knowledge that our Heavenly Father knows our needs."

–Dietrich Bonhoeffer

CHAPTER 8
WATCH, PRAY, VOTE

K nowledge is power, but only if it inspires action. After speaking on the racist roots of CRT and abortion, the question I hear most often is, "What can I do about it?" The problems facing our country seem so overwhelming that it can be difficult to know where to start. But that's what the enemy is counting on: God's people doing nothing.

Teaching about the end of the age, Jesus told His disciples, "Be always on the watch, and pray that you may be able to escape all that is about to happen, and that you may be able to stand before the Son of Man" (Luke 21:36). The first thing we must do is watch. One of the reasons that many believers feel as though things are spinning out of control so quickly is that they haven't been paying attention. In all fairness, the progressive movement has been pushing a culture of death, no-boundaries sex, and tribalism for more than a hundred years. They've just been chipping away at American culture a little piece at a time, hoping to chisel out a utopia of their own making. They've been playing the long game while most Christians have been content to live and let live, yielding the culture an issue at a time. But now that the darkness is flooding every corner of our society, the problems of progressivism are impossible to ignore. But they're not a recent development. It only seems that way because most of us haven't been paying attention.

Jesus said, "Be always on the watch." That means all the time—when things appear to be going well and when things most certainly are not. It makes no difference. We must be vigilant. We cannot let our guard down, not even for a moment. We have an enemy who will take every advantage he can; we must not give him any.

In the Old Testament, God appointed the prophet Ezekiel to be a watchman over His people:

Son of man, I have made you a watchman for the people of Israel; so hear the word I speak and give them warning from me. When I say to a wicked person, 'You will surely die,' and you do not warn them or speak out to dissuade them from their evil ways in order to save their life, that wicked person will die for their sin, and I will hold you accountable for their blood. But if you do warn the wicked person and they do not turn from their wickedness or from their evil ways, they will die for their sin; but you will have saved yourself. (Ezekiel 3:17–19)

In the ancient world, fortified cities were built with watchtowers so that watchmen could keep guard, peering into the distance to make sure no enemy approached unawares. At the first sign of trouble, the watchman was to alert the king so that defensive forces could be mustered and lives saved. Watchmen had to remain on high alert, focused and vigilant, during long shifts. A nighttime watch would require a watchman to keep a lookout until the break of dawn, since danger could come at any time.

All Christians are called to be watchmen, but pastors and other Christian leaders even especially. They must keep their eyes open and report what's coming in the distance. But for too long, our watchmen have either remained silent or been ignored.

Some of the silent watchmen are mum because they are not paying attention to the warning signs of culture flashing all around. Sadly, this is often because they have become so engrossed in the fading values of the day that they have forgotten their kingdom priorities. I am thinking here of pastors engrossed in celebrity Christian culture, which prioritizes platform and social media presence over God's Word and the care of individual souls.

Others who remain silent have themselves been deceived. They imagine the enemies storming the gates are really not so bad. They falsely believe that the best way to follow Christ in this world is to play nice with the forces that are attempting to upend Western culture along with its Judeo-Christian foundation. The Lord has a dire warning for the watchman who refuses to speak:

> But if the watchman sees the sword coming and does not blow the trumpet to warn the people and the sword comes and takes someone's life, that person's life be taken because of their sin, but I will hold the watchmen accountable for their blood. (Ezekiel 33:6).

These timid watchmen note that Jesus Himself said to turn the other cheek (Matthew 5:39). However, they're missing the part where Jesus said to love your neighbor (22:39). One of the best ways we can love our neighbors is by standing up for what is right and cultivating a society where people from every walk of life can flourish. CRT and abortion seek to sow enmity and destroy life. We will all be worse off if these progressive ideals are allowed to remain and grow.

Thankfully, not all of our watchmen remain silent. Many pastors and teachers do signal the danger that is coming. Some have been doing it for quite a long time. All too often, however, their warnings have been ignored and even brushed aside as counterproductive. For example, in 2008, Dr. James Dobson, then host of the popular *Focus on the Family* radio broadcast, sounded the alarm about the coming progressive agenda set to change America forever. Just weeks prior to the presidential election, Dobson released a fictional "Letter from 2012 in Obama's America."[1] In the letter, he lamented many radical changes to the nation, including the appointment of three liberal Supreme Court justices, the legalization of homosexual marriage, unfettered access to abortion, and single-payer healthcare.

Of course, not all of Dobson's predictions came to pass in Obama's first term, or even in his second. However, Dobson correctly marked the trajectory the Democrats were on. Looking at Dobson's predictions, he was right about a few key issues: gay marriage was legalized across all fifty states in a Supreme Court ruling (though not in 2010 but in 2015), and that change brought with it many religious freedom concerns that are still being worked out today. Homosexuals were permitted into the military without restriction (not in 2008 but in 2011). And Obama did appoint three Supreme Court justices (which would have shifted the balance of the court were it not for the Republican-controlled Senate's refusal to take up the nomination of Merrick Garland toward the end of Obama's second term). Even where specific predictions did not come true, the trendlines were—and still are—certainly there.[2]

At the time, many people thought Dobson was fear-mongering. They said he had put his personal political views ahead of the gospel and biblical teaching related to family issues. In February of 2009, Dobson stepped down as chairman of the board for Focus on the Family. In November of that year, he revealed that the board had asked him to resign. His final radio program aired shortly thereafter. Then, he launched a new ministry, the Dr. James Dobson Family Institute, and a new radio program, *Dr. James Dobson's Family Talk.*

A few months later, former NFL linebacker, pastor of Antioch Bible Church, and personal friend of Dobson, Ken Hutcherson, wrote:

> I think that Focus does have a new focus; an image change designed to make them accepted and well-liked rather than standing for righteousness in an unrighteous society. . . .
>
> The current emphasis at Focus is on being loved and understood. I have read the entire Bible from Genesis 1:1 through Revelation 22:21 – and while it says, "The truth shall set you free," nowhere does it say, "Sensitivity shall set you free." What set the Focus board free to take Dr. Dobson off the air? . . .
>
> It was, after all, the James Dobson radio program, not the Focus on the Family radio program. This board will regret its decision not to honor the founder of the ministry that God ordained. I have already had many tell me where their support will go. If the board members

have any guts at all, they will get this man back on the Focus radio program.

I love Dr. Dobson, and what I am saying he will never say. It may get him upset, but the board's decision must be discussed and challenged. I think the board has been misled and made a very unwise decision. One thing is for sure, in his humility, Dr. Dobson only wants to continue to speak the truth on the radio. Apparently, that truth has limited appeal to the new leadership at Focus.[3]

It is not my place to accuse the leadership of Focus on the Family of anything improper, nor is that my intention. Rather, I bring up Dobson's Letter from 2012 because it looks a lot like the sort of thing a good watchman ought to be doing. We might quibble over his presentation and his use of a fictional letter, but no one can say Dobson didn't try to warn us. The real problem was not with Dobson; it was with all who refused to listen. A watchman can scream and shout and wave his arms to tell us that danger is on the horizon, but if no one is paying attention, it makes no difference.

So how do we become watchmen? Theologian Karl Barth is often credited with saying that, as Christians, "We must hold the Bible in one hand and the newspaper in the other." I think Barth was onto something. We don't need to be able to peer into the future to be watchmen. We just need to understand current events in the light of Scripture. To do that, two things are required.

First, we must be committed students of God's Word, going deep to understand the original context of each passage and how the truths we read apply to our lives today. Those of us who are pastors must preach it faithfully, clearly, and without apology. There is tremendous power in expository preaching, especially when preaching through entire books of the Bible.

Second, we must know how to think biblically and critically about the news we read and watch, including how the story is framed and the likely bias of the source. Most importantly, with every story, we should learn to ask ourselves, *Does Scripture speak to this subject? Are there biblical principles that should inform my thinking?* We must also learn to see trends rather than isolated events. *Roe v. Wade* was a single Supreme Court decision, a moment in time that has altered the fabric of America, but it didn't appear out of thin air. There was a long train of social changes that made the decision possible. As believers, we must learn to see what is likely to come if we don't act.

THE KING HAD JUST ISSUED a decree that outlawed prayers directed toward anyone but himself. And when Daniel heard about it, "he went home to his upstairs room where the windows opened toward Jerusalem. Three times a day he got down on his knees and prayed, giving thanks to his God, just as he had done before" (Daniel 6:10).

Daniel was Jewish exile living in the land of Babylon, serving in the king's court as a wise man. Despite his position of power and influence, Daniel was loyal to the Lord. And so, it didn't matter if King Darius had made it a crime to pray; he would bow down toward the holy city of God and pray three times a day, no matter the consequences.

It didn't take long for those consequences to come. Daniel was thrown into a den of hungry lions, sentenced to certain death in one of the most horrifying ways imaginable. A stone was placed over the opening to the den to make sure there was no escape. But, of course, Daniel didn't die. An angel came and shut the mouths of the lions. The next morning, Darius arrived to find Daniel unharmed.

Have you ever thought about why Daniel took such a big risk, praying before an open window? He could have relaxed his prayer life for thirty days to play it safe, or at the very least, prayed in private. Instead, Daniel was bold in his prayers, unashamed to lift his voice and his heart up to the Lord. It was because Daniel knew that nothing in his life would mean anything without his connection to God. Jesus Himself would later say, "What good is it for someone to gain the whole world, yet forfeit their soul?" (Mark 8:36). Daniel knew the answer to this instinctively, so he chose to forego the world in order to be bold for God.

As Christians living in the West, our situation is not all that different from Daniel's. We, too, are surrounded by a pagan, decadent culture. We, too, have a choice to make: we can either serve the kingdoms of this world or the kingdom of our God. And while no one may be threatening to turn us into lion food, it still costs something to be bold for Jesus. Like Daniel, we need to be people of prayer, for if we lose our relationship with the Lord, nothing else really matters. We can fight to rid our schools and culture of CRT, but without God, we are lost. We can fight to overturn *Roe v. Wade* and advocate for policies that promote a culture of life, but if we take for granted the God who loves us, then we have only succeeded in restraining a measure of evil in this world while forsaking its King.

Prayer must be central in everything we do, and I'm not just saying that because it might sound pious or inspirational. The truth is, if we try to push back the darkness on our own—no matter how hard we work, no matter how strategic we are, and no matter how many people we convince—we will fail. The only way our culture will change is if God brings revival to our land. Without the Lord's help, we may succeed in pushing back the CRT agenda, but it will only be replaced with something even more vile and destructive. We might even end legalized abortion in America, once and for all, but a true culture of life can only flourish when people submit to the Author of life.

Not only do we need to be men and women of prayer, but we must teach our children to be prayer warriors as well. Contrary to what many people will tell you, we have freedom of religion in this country, and that includes our children. They have the right to pray in school, to read and study their Bible in school, and to share their faith. Period. Full stop. Yet how many of us push back when we're told that our public schools must maintain a separation of church and state? Read the Constitution. There's nothing in there about this famed "wall of separation between Church and State."

The phrase originated not in any official government document but in a letter Thomas Jefferson wrote to the Danbury Baptist Association of Danbury, Connecticut, dated January 1, 1802. The Baptists had written to Jefferson to congratulate him on his election to the office of president of the United States, but in their letter they relayed their concern over government encroachment on matters of religion. Jefferson replied to assure them that the First Amendment in the Bill of Rights recognized their right to practice their religion as their consciences dictated:

> Believing with you that religion is a matter which lies solely between man and his God; that he owes account to none other for his faith or his worship; that the legislative powers of government reach actions only and not opinions, I contemplate with sovereign reverence

that act of the whole American people which declared that their legislature should "make no law respecting an establishment of religion or prohibiting the free exercise thereof," thus building a wall of separation between Church and State.[4]

There is a wall of separation between Church and State, but it is not there to keep faith out of the public square or our public schools. Rather, it is there to keep the federal government from doing precisely what it is doing now: dictating how and when we practice our religion.

In order to be free people, we need to live like free people. We cannot allow the media or popular opinion to dictate how we live. To live in fear is not to really live at all. Daniel understood this. God had set him free, and so he lived out that freedom, even though he knew it might cost him his life. But for too long, too many Christians in the United States have been living in fear, afraid to stand up for what is right. They've silently agreed to keep their faith a private matter, retreated from the public square, and settled for a comfortable life rather than a kingdom life.

Sadly, many Christians have fallen for the lie that politeness is the same thing as goodness. They believe it's loving their neighbor when they remain silent instead of speaking truth that might be offensive. They have assumed that as a follower of Christ, they are supposed to lay down their rights. Of course, they are supposed to do just that—but at the feet of Jesus, not at the behest of the government.

You have a God-given right to love the Lord and serve Him. One of the things that sets America apart as a different kind of nation is that our founding documents recognize this right as unalienable. Now, more than ever, we need to exercise this right. We need to stand boldly as men and women of prayer—to give ourselves wholly and completely over to Him as we seek the good of all people by opposing racism in all its forms.

SAINT AUGUSTINE ONCE SAID, "Pray as though everything depended on God. Work as though everything depended on you." Of course, we know that everything *does* depend on God. Even so, the Lord has seen fit to use us as His instruments in this world. Knowing that, we must be good stewards of the resources, time, and talents He's given to us.

In prayer, we ask, as Jesus taught us, "your kingdom come, your will be done, on earth as it is in heaven" (Matthew 6:10). But when get up off our knees, it's time to live out that prayer. We are to be people who make this world a bit more like the kingdom with each decision we make and each moment of influence we are given. We are to be people who strive to see God's will done on earth just as it is in heaven. There ought to be no distance between our prayers and our actions.

There are voices among us who say we ought to keep our politics and our faith separated, so as not to offend would-be disciples of Christ. While it might sound as though there's wisdom in that approach, it betrays how Christian faith actually works. Jesus doesn't call us to church on Sundays or small group on Wednesdays; He calls us to follow Him each and every day of our lives. He calls us to give Him everything—including our politics. Rather than thinking of our political engagement as a separate category, it's better to think of it as an extension of our faith. What we believe should invariably spill over into how we vote.

The New Testament book of James offers this instruction to believers:

> Do not merely listen to the word, and so deceive yourselves. Do what it says. Anyone who listens to the word but does not do what it says is like someone who looks at his face in a mirror and, after looking at himself, goes away and immediately forgets what he looks like. But whoever looks intently into the perfect law that gives freedom, and continues in it—not forgetting what they have heard, but doing it—they will be blessed in what they do. (James 1:22–25)

As I read these words of wisdom, I can't help but think

of many believers today—black and white and every shade in between—who confess biblical truth with their lips but then go out into the world and engage in politics as though they have never read a word of Scripture.

To be sure, there is no perfect political party, and there are no perfect candidates either. We live in a fallen world populated by fallen human beings. Until Jesus returns in glory, we will have no perfect rulers. So, whenever we vote, we are voting for the lesser of two evils. That said, there is so little in the progressive agenda for a follower of Christ to cling to that it's astonishing to me that I continue to see otherwise faithful brothers and sisters vote for Leftist candidates.

One party is pro-life; the other is for abortion on demand. One party wants America to fulfill the dream of its founding—to be a place that recognizes "all men are created equal"; the other wants to rewrite the history books to pit one race against another. One party wants parents to be able to educate their children however they see fit; the other wants to keep God out of the schools, silence prayers in the classroom, and deconstruct the teachings of Scripture to fit their postmodern agenda.

Voting doesn't just happen on the second Tuesday in November every four years. Voting, in the truest sense, happens every day. We vote with the choices we make, the words we speak, and the questions we ask. As Christians, we are ambassadors for God's kingdom, and we're never off-duty. We must remain engaged throughout the political process every day of the year. It starts at the grassroots level, whenever we speak the truth in love to family, friends, and neighbors. It continues and grows when we stand for what we believe in our communities, our churches, and our workplaces. It shakes the culture when we refuse to take in the lies being breathed out by Hollywood, Silicon Valley, and corporate media newsrooms. And it changes the direction of the nation when we vote our conscience at the polls.

One of the ways we vote every day is by choosing how we spend our dollars. Every time you swipe your card or check out online, you're either reinforcing the status quo or pressing for change. Take some time and do your research to find what companies espouse values you share and what companies are pursuing a woke agenda. Look up which brands financially support organizations like Planned Parenthood and Black Lives Matter, and then choose where you shop accordingly. While you're at it, move away from social media platforms that censor free speech or shun traditional American values.

While it would be extremely difficult to completely avoid supporting companies that veer to the Left, every dollar shifted away is one less dollar that can be used to promote philosophies and behavior that are tearing our country apart. The point is not to make grocery shopping political; it's to actively pursue the kind of world you want to live in. And your dollars are one way to vote for it.

There is another way to vote, and it's arguably the most powerful and consequential vote you will ever cast: it's the decision you make about where your child will be educated. To put it mildly, public schools are no longer safe places for our kids. I want to urge you, if there are any other options for your child's education, please pursue them. Is there an affordable Christian school in your area? Consider sending your child there. Do you have the flexibility to homeschool? You'll be amazed at the resources that exist to equip you to teach at home, and I think you'll be surprised by just how wonderful the experience can be for both of you. If neither of those options are viable, check to see if your child is eligible for a charter school in your area. Many charter schools, while still funded by taxpayer dollars, are not tied to the standard curriculum being used in most public schools. And if your child must attend a public school, be sure you are supplementing their education at home. Also, before your son or daughter leaves for school each morning, let them know you will be proud of them when they stand boldly for Jesus in a place where He is no longer welcome.

For many years, some Christian leaders argued that while homeschooling and private Christian education were fine for some, our public schools needed Christian students to shine the light of Jesus Christ. While it's certainly true that our public schools need more light, I do not believe that our children should be asked to be that light while receiving an education that is divorced from God and that will stunt their ability to learn. Instead, men and women who love Jesus should run for local school boards and speak up for what is right, as should Christian teachers and faculty members. It may be costly, and change may come slowly, but the cost of doing nothing is simply too great.

Lastly, let's not forget that one of the reasons socialism is so easy to promote in our schools is that our public school system is itself socialized. We should not be surprised, then, at the gradual but steady downward slide in quality education and freedom in our schools; that's always what happens when you centralize something and give more power to the government. The problem of socialism cannot be solved with a few tweaks or personnel changes. The problem is down deep in the roots, so the roots must be extricated from the ground. No matter how stubbornly they refuse to move, they must be pulled from their place. The answer is to replace government-controlled education with parent-led education. We must have true school choice.

How many young minds would be set free if moms and dads had the ability to send their kids to the school of their choice? How many parents of children currently in private schools could be freed from paying for school twice—once through local school taxes and again in tuition? How quickly would underperforming schools turn around when suddenly faced with stiff competition? And how soon would anti-American, anti-Christian curriculum change if parents made the ultimate decision about what their child studied? This is the power of school choice—so be sure to let your representatives on every level know it's an issue you care deeply about. And be sure to vote for candidates who are not beholden to the teacher's unions.

IT'S FITTING that the way we bring about change is to watch, pray, and vote. This country was founded on those principles. Our Founding Fathers were great observers, not only of current events, but of history, and they knew that replacing a king with a president would do little to stem the tide of tyranny, so they created a system of government filled with checks and balances. In other words, they were watchmen who saw what would come if they didn't proceed with great wisdom.

They were also men of prayer, committing their endeavors and this nation to the Lord. Consider how Benjamin Franklin made an appeal for prayer at the Constitutional Convention, recognizing the significance of the task before them:

> Before I sit down, Mr. President, I will suggest another matter; and I am really surprised that it has not been proposed by some other member at an earlier period of our deliberations. I will suggest, Mr. President, that

propriety of nominating and appointing, before we separate, a chaplain to this Convention, whose duty it shall be uniformly to assemble with us, and introduce the business of each day by and address to the Creator of the universe, and the Governor of all nations, beseeching Him to preside in our council, enlighten our minds with a portion of heavenly wisdom, influence our hearts with a love of truth and justice, and crown our labors with complete and abundant success![5]

Lastly, the Founding Fathers believed that we should be a nation of the people, by the people, and for the people. Voting, therefore, runs in the veins of every true American. We were not meant to be a people who solved their problems with violence or shouting matches. We were once a nation that debated issues and competed in the marketplace of ideas. We then went to the ballot box to set a course for the next season.

We must return to these first principles. We must become men and women who care enough about our communities, our children, and our country to watch, pray, and vote. Most of all, we must be people who love all life—every race and color—and who see all mankind, born and unborn, as one blood and equally valuable. It's the only way forward.

Connect with John K. Amanchukwu Sr.

WEBSITE

www.johnamanchukwu.com/

SPEAKING VIDEOS

Love Life California Conference

1. www.youtube.com/watch?v=YD86JGIwTFM
2. www.youtube.com/watch?v=SdiHLrepPXA

SOCIAL MEDIA

LinkedIn: www.linkedin.com/in/john-k-amanchukwu-sr-84202a29/

Facebook: https://www.facebook.com/john.amanchukwu

Instagram: https://www.instagram.com/revwutruth/

NOTES

1. KEEP YOUR EYE ON THE BALL

1. Maanvi Singh, "George Floyd told officers 'I can't breathe' more than 20 times, transcripts show," *The Guardian,* July 9, 2020, https://www.theguardian.com/us-news/2020/jul/08/george-floyd-police-killing-transcript-i-cant-breathe.
2. Evan Hill, Ainara Tiefenthäler, Ainara Tiefenthäler, Christiaan Triebert, Drew Jordan, Haley Willis, and Robin Stein, "How George Floyd Was Killed in Police Custody," *The New York Times,* May 31, 2020, https://www.nytimes.com/2020/05/31/us/george-floyd-investigation.html.
3. Gavrilo David, "Why Derek Chauvin May Get Off His Murder Charge," *Medium,* June 11, 2020, https://medium.com/@gavrilo-david/why-derek-chauvin-may-get-off-his-murder-charge-2e2ad8d0911.
4. Amy Forliti, "Chauvin to appeal conviction, sentence in Floyd's death," *AP News,* September 23, 2021, https://apnews.com/article/death-of-george-floyd-trials-minneapolis-fa59d91c63573a65ba31927ce2e076b7.
5. Paul Joseph Watson, "Alternate Juror on Chauvin Trial Says She Feared Riots, People Turning Up At Her Home," *Summit News,* April 23, 2021, https://summit.news/2021/04/23/alternate-juror-on-chauvin-trial-says-she-feared-riots-people-turning-up-at-her-home/.
6. M Dowling, "Chauvin juror exposes his own potential misconduct," *Independent Sentinel,* May 3, 2021, https://www.independentsentinel.com/chauvin-juror-exposes-his-own-potential-misconduct/.
7. Eric Paulsen, "10 Facts about the Holdomor Genocide," The Borgen Project, https://borgenproject.org/holodomor-genocide/.
8. Anne Applebaum, "How Stalin Hid Ukraine's Famine From the World," *The Atlantic,* October 13, 2017, https://www.theatlantic.com/in-

ternational/archive/2017/10/red-famine-anne-applebaum-ukraine-soviet-union/542610/.

9. Brian Flood, Joseph Wulfsohn, "CNN did not mention on-air David Dorn, retired St. Louis police captain killed by looters," June 3, 2020, Foxnews.com, https://www.foxnews.com/media/cnn-david-dorn-retired-police-captain-killed-st-louis.

10. Sam Dorman, "What is critical race theory?" Fox News, May 14, 2021, https://www.foxnews.com/us/what-is-critical-race-theory.

11. See, for example, Walter E. Williams, "Correct English Grammar Is 'Racist'," The Daily Signal, September 11, 2019, https://www.education-views.org/correct-english-grammar-is-racist/; see also Lionel Du Cane, "College Professor Calls SpongeBob a 'Violent,' 'Racist' Colonizer," National File, October 21, 2019, https://nationalfile.com/college-profes-sor-calls-spongebob-a-violent-racist-colonizer/

12. The Heritage Foundation, "How to Identify Critical Race Theory: Knowing Critical Race Theory When You See It and Fighting It When You Can," Accessed January 10, 2022, https://www.heritage.org/civil-society/heritage-explains/how-identify-critical-race-theory.

13. Kamala Harris (@KamalaHarris), "There's a big difference between equality and equity," Twitter video, November 1, 2020, https://twitter.com/KamalaHarris/status/1322963321994289154.

14. Star Parker, ed., "The Effects of Abortion on the Black Community," Center for Urban Renewal and Education Policy Report, June 2015, https://www.congress.gov/115/meeting/house/106562/witnesses/HHRG-115-JU10-Wstate-ParkerS-20171101-SD001.pdf.

15. Brenna Lewis, "Senator Rand Paul Urges the Smithsonian to Remove Bust of Racist Planned Parenthood Founder Margaret Sanger," Students for Life Action, May 20, 2021, https://www.stu-dentsforlifeaction.org/senator-rand-paul-urges-the-smithsonian-to-remove-bust-of-racist-planned-parenthood-founder-margaret-sanger/.

16. Eric Bradner, Sarah Mucha, and Arlette Saenz, "Biden: 'If you have a problem figuring out whether you're for me or Trump, then you ain't black,'" CNN.com, May 22, 2020, https://www.cnn.com/2020/05/22/pol-itics/biden-charlamagne-tha-god-you-aint-black/index.html.

Ruth Igielnik, Scott Keeter, and Hannah Hartig, "Behind Biden's 2020

Victory," Pew Research Center, June 30, 2021, https://www.pewresearch.org/politics/2021/06/30/behind-bidens-2020-victory/.

18. "The Most Segregated Hour in America - Martin Luther King Jr.," YouTube Video, 0:52, April 29, 2014, https://www.youtube.com/watch?v=1q88IgiL_d8.

2. NOTHING NEW UNDER THE SUN

1. History.com Editors, "Little Rock Nine," History, updated February 10, 2020, https://www.history.com/topics/black-history/central-high-school-integration.

2. Fiza Pirani, "7 things to know about the Little Rock Nine," *The Atlanta Journal-Constitution*, February 20, 2018, https://www.ajc.com/news/national/things-know-about-the-little-rock-nine/ysmvHfrh6yNqkmqtkJkmMO/.

3. Dustin Barnes, "Columbia University offering graduation ceremonies based on race, ethnicity, income status," *USA Today*, March 16, 2021, https://www.usatoday.com/story/news/education/2021/03/16/columbia-university-offers-graduation-ceremonies-based-race-income/4716586001/.

4. Karsten Schneider, "New York University moves to implement racial segregation in student dorms," World Socialist Web Site, August 24, 2020, https://www.wsws.org/en/articles/2020/08/24/nyur-a24.html.

5. Ibram X. Kendi, "How Should We React to White Student Unions," Diverse Issues in Higher Education, Updated August 16, 2013, https://www.diverseeducation.com/students/article/15093543/how-should-we-react-to-white-student-unions.

6. Dion J. Pierre, "Demands for Segregated Housing at Williams College Are Not News," *National Review*, May 8, 2019, https://www.nationalreview.com/2019/05/american-colleges-segregated-housing-graduation-ceremonies/.

7. Martin Luther King Jr. as quoted in James Lankford and Tim Scott, "'People Who Are Different Are Not the Problem in America'," *The Atlantic*, January 12, 2018, https://www.theatlantic.com/politics/archive/2018/01/mlk-today/550466/.

8. Jeff Wallenfeldt, "Wilmington coup and massacre," Britannica, Updated November 3, 2021, https://www.britannica.com/event/Wilmington-coup-and-massacre/additional-info#history.

9. Kim Parker and Kiley Hurst, "Growing share of Americans say they want more spending on police in their area," Pew Research Center, October 26, 2021, https://www.pewresearch.org/fact-tank/2021/10/26/growing-share-of-americans-say-they-want-more-spending-on-police-in-their-area/.

10. "Shaping the Future: Indoctrinating Youth," United States Holocaust Memorial Museum, Accessed January 19, 2022, https://www.ushmm.org/propaganda/themes/indoctrinating-youth/.

11. Ibid.

12. William Cronon, "'Only Connect...': The Goals of a Liberal Education," *The American Scholar*, Volume 67, No. 4, Autumn 1998, https://www.williamcronon.net/writing/only_connect.html.

13. "What's Wrong with the 1619 Project," YouTube Video, 5:55, November 30, 2020, https://www.youtube.com/watch?v=OrqFbyTABmQ.

14. Ibid.

15. "Hitler Speaks to the Reichstag on the Jewish Question: Selected Extracts from Adolf Hitler's *The Jewish Question* speech, delivered before the Reichstag in Berlin, Germany - January 30, 1939," Holocaust Education & Archive Research Team, Accessed January 18, 2022, http://www.holocaustresearchproject.org/holoprelude/jewishquestion.html.

16. "US States – Ranked by Population 2021," World Population Review, Accessed January 18, 2022, https://worldpopulationreview.com/states.

17. Walt Blackman, "Abortion: The overlooked tragedy for black Americans," *Arizona Capitol Times*, February 25, 2020, https://azcapitoltimes.com/news/2020/02/25/abortion-the-overlooked-tragedy-for-black-americans/.

18. Ibid.

19. Ibid.

20. Kristan Hawkins, "Remove statues of Margaret Sanger, Planned Parenthood founder tied to eugenics and racism," *USA Today*, July 23, 2020, https://www.usatoday.com/story/opinion/2020/07/23/racism-eugenics-margaret-sanger-deserves-no-honors-column/5480192002/.

21. "Abby Johnson: Seeing an Ultrasound Abortion Made Me Leave Planned Parenthood | Kirk Cameron on TBN," YouTube Video, 14:05, January 17, 2021, https://www.youtube.com/watch?v=AkINeP-ibXI.

22. Ibid.

3. MURDER, SHE WROTE

1. Carrie Mumah, "Planned Parenthood of Greater New York Announces Intent to Remove Margaret Sanger's Name from NYC Health Center," Planned Parenthood of Greater New York, July 21, 2020, https://www.plannedparenthood.org/planned-parenthood-greater-new-york/about/news/planned-parenthood-of-greater-new-york-announces-intent-to-remove-margaret-sangers-name-from-nyc-health-center.

2. Darrah @ Planned Parenthood, "Planned Parenthood's Reckoning with Margaret Sanger," Planned Parenthood of the Pacific Southwest, April 23, 2021, https://www.plannedparenthood.org/planned-parenthood-pacific-southwest/blog/planned-parenthoods-reckoning-with-margaret-sanger.

3. John J. Conley, S. J., "Margaret Sanger was a eugenicist. Why are we still celebrating her?" *America: The Jesuit Review*, November 27, 2017, https://www.americamagazine.org/politics-society/2017/11/27/margaret-sanger-was-eugenicist-why-are-we-still-celebrating-her.

4. Brian Clowes, PhD, "The Strange World of Margaret Sanger's *Birth Control Review*: Part I," Human Life International, April 18, 2017, https://www.hli.org/resources/sangers-birth-control-review-part-i/.

5. John J. Conley, S. J., Ibid.

6. Margaret Sanger, as quoted in Mary Anne Dion, "Hitler, The Ku Klux Klan, and Margaret Sanger," letter to the editor, *The Courier-Herald*, April 10, 2019, https://www.courierherald.com/letters/hitler-the-ku-klux-klan-and-margaret-sanger/.

7. Margaret Sanger. "Birth Control and Women's Health." *Birth Control Review*, Volume I, Number 12 (December 1917), 7.

8. Brian Clowes, PhD, Ibid.

9. Ibid.

10. Julian Huxley. "America Revisited III: The Negro Problem." *The Spectator*, November 29, 1924.

11. Jennifer Latson, "Why Birth Control Pioneer Margaret Sanger Kept Getting Arrested," *Time*, October 16, 2015, https://time.com/4065338/margaret-sanger-clinic-history/.

12. Margaret Sanger, "Letter from Margaret Sanger to Dr. C. J. Gamble," Genius, Accessed January 23, 2022, https://genius.com/Margaret-sanger-letter-from-margaret-sanger-to-dr-cj-gamble-annotated.

13. Ibid.

14. Mary Anne Dion, Ibid.

15. CWALAC Staff, "The Negro Project: Margaret Sanger's Eugenic Plan for Black Americans," Concerned Women for America Legislative Action Committee, May 1, 2001, https://concernedwomen.org/the-negro-project-margaret-sangers-eugenic-plan-for-black-americans/.

16. Ibid.

17. George S. Schuyler, "Quantity or Quality," *The Birth Control Review*, June 1932, 166.

18. CWALAC Staff, Ibid.

4. THE ROLE OF THE BLACK MINISTER

1. Jesse Jackson, "The Texas Taliban wing of the Republican Party," *Chicago Sun-Times*, September 3, 2021, https://chicago.suntimes.com/columnists/2021/9/3/22656493/the-texas-taliban-wing-of-the-republican-party.

2. Jesse Jackson, "How we respect life is the over-riding moral issue," *Right to Life News*, January, 1977, https://groups.csail.mit.edu/mac/users/rauch/nvp/consistent/jackson.html.

3. Colman McCarthy, "Jackson's Reversal on Abortion, *The Washington Post*, May 21, 1988, https://www.washingtonpost.com/archive/opinions/1988/05/21/jacksons-reversal-on-abortion/dd9e1637-020d-447b-9329-95ec67e41fd5/.

4. Ibid.

John D. Barry et al., *Faithlife Study Bible* (Bellingham, WA: Lexham Press, 2012, 2016), Mt 18:22.

5. THE ROLE OF THE WHITE MINISTER

1. Cassandra Fairbanks, "Charlotte Black Lives Matter Rioters March Down the Street Chanting 'F-ck Your Jesus,' Cover Street Preacher With Silly String (VIDEOS)," Gateway Pundit, August 25, 2020, https://www.thegatewaypundit.com/2020/08/charlotte-black-lives-matter-rioters-march-street-chanting-f-ck-jesus-cover-street-preacher-silly-string-videos/.

2. "Billy Graham on Race Relations," YouTube Video, 1:59, February 22, 2018, https://www.youtube.com/watch?v=74zHUqC99cE&t=61s.

3. Edward Gilbreath, "History in the Making—Billy Graham Had a Dream," *Christian History*, Issue No. 47, 1995, https://christianhistoryinstitute.org/magazine/article/history-in-the-making-billy-graham-had-a-dream.

4. Mike Gonzalez, "What the Media Doesn't Want You to Know About 2020's Record Murder Spike," The Heritage Foundation, October 7, 2021, https://www.heritage.org/crime-and-justice/commentary/what-the-media-doesnt-want-you-know-about-2020s-record-murder-spike.

5. According to FBI statistics, in 2016 there were 2,570 murders in which the victim and the offender were both black. That's compared to 553 where the perpetrator was black and the victim was white, and 243 where the murderer was white and the victim was black. See Andrew C. McCarthy, "Understanding Black-on-Black Murders," *National Review*, June 25, 2020, https://www.nationalreview.com/corner/understating-black-on-black-murders/.

6. See, for example, Amina Khan, "Getting killed by police is a leading cause of death for young black men in America," *Los Angeles Times,* August 16, 2019, https://www.latimes.com/science/story/2019-08-15/police-shootings-are-a-leading-cause-of-death-for-black-men. This headline ignores the very findings it reveals: that the number one cause of death for black men in their mid- to late-twenties was "assault," with a 94.2 percent mortality rate, while police violence had a 3.4% rate. Obviously 3.4% is still unacceptable, but it is a strange thing that the headline wasn't about assault.

7. Mark Campbell, "Five Fears That Keep Pastors from Preaching about Abortion," Focus on the Family, June 15, 2018, https://www.focusonthe-

family.com/pro-life/five-fears-that-keep-pastors-from-preaching-about-abortion/.

8. Ibid.

9. Cole Brown, "Jesus Is Not Colorblind," The Gospel Coalition, March 20, 2018, https://www.thegospelcoalition.org/article/jesus-isnt-colorblind/.

10. Latasha Morrison, *Be the Bridge* (Colorado Springs: Waterbrook, 2019), 23.

6. STOCKHOLM SYNDROME

1. Christopher Klein, "Stockholm Syndrome: The True Story of Hostages Loyal to Their Captor," History, April 9, 2019, https://www.history.com/news/stockholm-syndrome.

2. Ismail K. White and Chryl N. Laird, "Why are Blacks Democrats?" Princeton University Press, February 25, 2020, https://press.princeton.edu/ideas/why-are-blacks-democrats.

3. Frederick Douglass, "What, to a Slave, Is the Fourth of July?" (July 5, 1852), Black Past, January 24, 2007, https://www.blackpast.org/african-american-history/speeches-african-american-history/1852-frederick-douglass-what-slave-fourth-july/#:~:text=What%2C%20to%20the%20Ameri-can%20slave,he%20is%20the%20constant%20victim.

4. Ibid.

5. D. H. Dilbeck, "The Radical Christian Faith of Frederick Douglass," *Christianity Today,* December 21, 2017, https://www.christianitytoday.com/ct/2018/january-february/frederick-douglass-at-200-remember-ing-his-radical-christian.html.

6. Manning Johnson, *Color, Communism and Common Sense,* "Chapter Two: Subverting Negro Churches," Accessed February 12, 2022, https://manningjohnson.org/book/CCCS_2.html.

7. "Dinesh D'Souza Dishes On Cenk Uygur And Debate Hacks (Uncut Web Extended) | Louder With Crowder," YouTube Video, 35:31, August 19, 2016, https://www.youtube.com/watch?v=rrTcRbuvYXA.

7. WHAT ABOUT THE CHILDREN?

1. Steven Ertelt, "63,459,781 Babies Have Been Killed in Abortions Since Roe v. Wade in 1973," LifeNews.com, January 7, 2022, https://www.life-news.com/2022/01/07/63459781-babies-have-been-killed-in-abortions-since-roe-v-wade-in-1973/.

2. Joseph Simonson, "Some examples of critical race theory in schools," *Washington Examiner*, April 25, 2021, https://www.washingtonexamin-er.com/news/some-examples-of-critical-race-theory-in-schools.

3. Jennifer Kabbany, "Yes, CRT is taught in K-12 schools. Here's how." The College Fix, November 8, 2021, https://www.thecollegefix.-com/yes-crt-is-taught-in-k-12-schools-heres-how/.

4. "Examples of CRT," Defend Our Kids, Accessed February 13, 2022, https://defendourkids.org/examples-of-crt/.

5. Phil Shiver, "At least 30 school districts use children's book that teaches 'whiteness' is an evil contract with the devil," Blaze Media, July 9, 2021, https://www.theblaze.com/news/childrens-book-white-ness-contract-with-devil.

6. Jonathan Butcher and Mike Gonzalez, "Keep Racist Critical Race Theory Ideology Out of K–12 Classrooms," The Heritage Foundation, April 22, 2021, https://www.heritage.org/education/commentary/keep-racist-critical-race-theory-ideology-out-k-12-classrooms.

7. "What is Paideia?" Association of Classical Christian Schools, Accessed February 14, 2022, https://classicalchristian.org/what-is-paideia/.

8. The liberal arts are "liberal," in the sense that they "liberate" and should not be confused with the political or theological liberalism of today.

9. Robert Knight, "Socialism, Howard Zinn and his fake history," *The Washington Times,* January 5, 2020, https://www.washingtontimes.-com/news/2020/jan/5/socialism-howard-zinn-and-his-fake-history/.

10. "Historians Weigh In On The Confederate Statue Debate: The Torch Podcast: An Interview with Allen Guelzo, PhD and Edward O'Don-nell, PhD," The Great Courses Daily, October 17, 2017.

11. Paul Bond, "Nearly 40 Percent of U.S. Gen Zs, 30 Percent of Young

Christians Identify as LGBTQ, Poll Shows," *Newsweek*, October 20, 2021,   https://www.newsweek.com/nearly-40-percent-us-gen-zs-30-percent-christians-identify-lgbtq-poll-shows-1641085.

12. Beth Baumann, "WATCH: Drag Queen Story Hour Is Back Thanks To A Partnership Between NYC Department Of Education And PBS," The Daily Wire, May 20, 2021, https://www.dailywire.com/news/watch-drag-queen-story-hour-is-back-thanks-to-a-partnership-between-nyc-department-of-education-and-pbs.

13. Ibid.

14. WND News Service, "8th-graders get assigned to list their favorite sex acts like pizza toppings," WND, February 9, 2022, https://www.wnd.com/2022/02/8th-graders-get-assigned-list-favorite-sex-acts-like-pizza-toppings/.

15. Ibid.

16. Ibid.

8. WATCH, PRAY, VOTE

1. The full text of Dr. Dobson's letter is no longer available on any active website, but it has been archived. The full text is available here: https://web.archive.org/web/20081031013511/http://focusfamac-tion.edgeboss.net/download/focusfamaction/pdfs/10-22-08_2012let-ter.pdf

2. For example, Dobson referred to a fictional Freedom of Choice Act that made abortion the law of the land, no longer just by Supreme Court decision, thus making any attempt to overturn Roe v. Wade null and void. He mentioned that bans on partial birth abortions were removed in all fifty states. While that hasn't happened, New York State has legalized infanticide with the passage of the so-called Reproductive Health Act in 2019.

3. Ken Hutcherson, "I lost my focus on the family," WND, March 8, 2010, https://www.wnd.com/2010/03/127297/.

4. "Jefferson's Letter to the Danbury Baptists: The Draft and Recently Discovered Text" Library of Congress, Accessed February 20, 2022, https://www.loc.gov/loc/lcib/9806/danpost.html.

5. "Franklin's Appeal for Prayer at the Constitutional Convention," Wall-Builders, December 31, 2016, https://wallbuilders.com/franklins-appeal-prayer-constitutional-convention/.

ACKNOWLEDGMENTS

I want to acknowledge my wife, Crystal, and our three beautiful children. I pray that this book is the first of many to come from our family. I would not have been able to complete this project without your support, excitement, and encouragement.

I want to acknowledge my spiritual father, mentor and father-in-law, Bishop Patrick L. Wooden, Sr., for your example and instruction in life and holiness. Thank you for your steadfastness in doctrine. You continually demonstrate the importance of addressing the issues of our day with the gospel of Jesus Christ. Your support means the world to me. You are the G.O.A.T. and a servant is not greater than his master! I'm honored to be your understudy.

I want to acknowledge my mother, Carolyn Weeks, for her strength and tenacity. Your sincere love for Christ has impacted my life from childhood to today. I want to acknowledge my father, Joseph Amanchukwu, for constantly raising the standard and pushing me beyond my comfort zone.

I want to acknowledge and thank Jim and Betsy Duncan for your support while finishing my Master's program at Liberty University. I want to recognize my mother-in-law, First Lady Pamela Wooden: You have always been a true supporter of me from the beginning, thank you for your love, care and concern for me and my family. To my siblings (Chris, Joey, and Angela), Justin Reeder, Josh Kappes, and my Love Life family, the Happy Warriors, Margaret Hamilton and my church family for your support and encouragement along the way.

ABOUT THE AUTHOR

John is a graduate of North Carolina State University, where he played football under Coach Chuck Amato. John received a master's degree from Liberty University in Christian Ministry. He has been a youth and college pastor for fifteen years. Over the  past four years, John has led a 40-week prayer walk for Love Life at one of the busiest abortion clinics in the Southeast.

John has appeared on stage with many notable persons including: Nick Vujicic, Lila Rose, Kirk Cameron, Colton Dixon, David Daleiden, Bishop Patrick Wooden, Sr., Daniel Ritchie, Seth Gruber, Dr. Anthony Levatino, Jack Hibbs, Lt. Gov. Mark Robinson, and Dan Forest to name a few.

His audiences include: NC Right to Life, Wolf Pack Club, California Unite for Life Conference-2021, Love Life for Live Action, Calvary Chapel, Wake County Republican

Convention, Family Research Council, Parents for Educational Freedom, many churches across the nation, and Kirk Cameron's Campfire Revival Tour-2021.

He has been featured on WRAL-TV, Raleigh, NC, appeared on many podcasts, and his articles have been published in the News and Observer, Raleigh, NC., Civitas, and The Heritage Foundation.

He has been married to his wife Crystal for 14 years, and they have three children.

CPSIA information can be obtained
at www.ICGtesting.com
Printed in the USA
LVHW050937100722
723069LV00003B/6

9 780578 395173